# AUTHENTIC VICTOR
# FASHION PATTER

## A Complete Lady's Wardrobe

Edited by
# Kristina Harris

## DOVER PUBLICATIONS, INC.
Mineola, New York

*Bibliographical Note*

*Authentic Victorian Fashion Patterns: A Complete Lady's Wardrobe,* first published by Dover Publications, Inc., in 1999, is a selection of patterns from the following issues of *The Voice of Fashion:*
Vol. V, No. 18, Fall 1890; Vol. V, No. 19, Winter 1890–91; and Vol. V, No. 20, Spring 1891—all published by Goldsberry, Doran & Nelson, Chicago, Illinois.
Vol. VII, No. 28, Spring 1893; Vol. VIII, No. 29, Summer 1893; Vol. VIII, No. 32, Spring 1894; Vol. IX, No. 36, Spring 1895; and Vol. X, No. 39, Winter 1896—all published by Goldsberry & Doran, Chicago, Illinois.

*Library of Congress Cataloging-in-Publication Data*

Harris, Kristina.
    Authentic Victorian fashion patterns : a complete lady's wardrobe / Kristina Harris.
        p.     cm.
    Selected patterns from various issues of the Voice of fashion published in the 1890s.
    ISBN 0-486-40721-7 (pbk.)
    1. Dressmaking—Patterns.  2. Costume—United States—History—19th century.  I. Title.
TT520.H278     1999
646.4'78    21—dc21                                                    99-045684

Manufactured in the United States of America
Dover Publications, Inc., 31 East 2nd Street, Mineola, N.Y. 11501

# INTRODUCTION

"The society woman must have one or two velvet dresses which cannot cost less than $500 each," author and social reformer James McCabe reported in the late 19th century. "She must possess thousands of dollars' worth of laces. . . . Walking dresses cost from $50 to $300; ball dresses are frequently imported from Paris at a cost of from $500 to $1,000. . . . Then there are traveling dresses in black silk, in pongee, velour, in piqué, which range in price from $75 to $175. Then there are evening robes in Swiss muslin, robes in linen for the garden and croquet playing, dresses for horse races and for yacht races . . . dresses for breakfast and for dinner, dresses for receptions and for parties. . . ." None of the garments could be ready-made, and all came from a fine American dressmaker, if not a European couturier.

But the average, middle-class American woman could revel in no such luxury. Whenever she could, she pinched her pennies by making her own underwear. This not only saved her from having to pay a dressmaker for the task, it also protected her from inferior, ready-made underclothes. She might even try to sew some of her own clothing—but with the children's clothes to sew, plus a myriad of other pressing household duties, she usually left the making of her wardrobe to a dressmaker.

Most American women brought fashion plates (from one of the many middle-class fashion magazines available by the 1890s) to her local dressmaker; the dressmaker customized a chosen outfit according to her skills and her customer's desires. She could then either draft her own pattern, use the sewing pattern her client purchased through a fashion magazine, or consult a dressmaker's journal like *The Voice of Fashion*, which provided scaled patterns that could either be copied exactly, or adjusted to the customer's wants. If there was no dressmaker in town, or if a lady could not afford one, her next best source was a local seamstress—a housewife who took in sewing part time.

For many women, one new dress a season was all that could be afforded; some women felt fortunate to be able to have one new dress a year. It was fabric, not labor, that was usually the most expensive factor in creating a new dress. In 1890, *The American Woman* noted that while silks were still *the* fashionable fabrics, they would "not come into too general use because of their high price—the average being $7.50 a yard, and from this upward indefinitely. . . ." Even the

staunchly middle-class Sears, Roebuck and Company catalog featured a sateen described as "a near approach to the silk goods in appearance" that was still 20¢ a yard. This may seem affordable, but when one considers that an average 1890s dress could require four yards for the skirt (and, if it had large sleeves, another four to six yards, plus additional yardage for the rest of the bodice), it's easy to see how the fabric for a single basic housedress could run upwards of $2 to $3.

Of course, fabric was just one part of the expense. Facings, linings, interlinings, and boning were all necessary as well. According to *The American Woman*, highly decorative buttons were not only used as fastenings on some dresses, but were also "the favored trimming . . . and often come as high as $50 for a set of six buttons."

Finally, labor had to be considered. For a busy housewife (still using sad irons, a hand-cranked washing machine, a gas or wooden stove, and other archaic housekeeping devices used previous to the advent of electricity), it was usually worthwhile to hire someone else to do the actual sewing. Still, it was a cost not to be taken lightly. One magazine expressed great worry over the newest fashion of "befrilling and befurbelowing," hoping that it would "not keep on increasing; the labor and consequent expense of the dressmaking must naturally increase at the same rate." *The Voice of Fashion* itself noted that while "there is a great appearance of simplicity in the making up of spring dresses . . . the actual cost of these modern dresses is something beyond what had been even thought of hitherto . . . and is sometimes . . . a small fortune." In 1891, Hannah Ditzler, a middle-class Illinoian, wrote that her seamstress charged her $6 in labor alone for a plain woolen suit.

A ready-made dress from one of the new mail order catalogs could cost half of what a dressmaker- or seamstress-made dress would. It would not, however, fit the figure like a second skin, which was a necessity in Victorian fashions; therefore, even a less expensive ready-made dress had to be altered for fit. Because of these considerations, the job of many dressmakers and seamstresses was often to re-make older garments (for which patterns still came in handy).

Still, even though a moderate dressmaker-made dress ran about $10 (which was about the average middle-class man's weekly salary), the woman of the 1890s required more than just a few garments.

Victorian dressing was, after all, all about appearing appropriate during every situation—and Victorian society had fairly strict rules about just what was appropriate.

Beginning the moment she woke up in the morning, every Victorian lady required not just a nightgown, but also a wrapper. Wrappers (or tea gowns as they were sometimes called) were worn in the boudoir, to breakfast, and during private leisure hours. After breakfasting, the proper American woman then changed into a morning dress, which varied from any other type of dress primarily in its simplicity in design. The dress' hem could be short, but often touched the floor in front and at the sides, with a train no longer than six inches in the back.

A walking dress was required for walking into town or shopping; this usually featured more trimming than a morning dress, and always had a "short skirt." In the 1890s, this meant either instep length (two inches from the floor) or short round or clearing length (one inch from the floor). During the day, she might also require a visiting dress—a slightly more elaborate dress in a "round" length (just touching the floor at front, sides, and back). A housedress, which was usually made of washable material and trimming, was worn at home, and, depending upon how practical it was, could be either instep length or feature a slight train.

In addition, a dinner dress (touching the floor all around, and usually featuring a train of up to ten inches), and at least one version of its more splendid sister, the evening dress, was also required. Then there were riding habits for lady equestrians, tennis dresses for the typically active turn-of-the-century woman, bathing suits, bicycling and gym suits, et cetera. A proper middle-class woman's wardrobe of dress ran upwards of $80—though a good number of women could, and did, make do with less.

But this was only a part of the Victorian woman's wardrobe expense; she still had to be supplied with undergarments and accessories. These, according to middle-class fashion magazines of the era, included at least a half dozen chemises, a dozen pairs of drawers, nine petticoats, one to five flannel petticoats, nine camisoles, a dozen pairs of cotton stockings, three pairs silk stockings, two dozen handkerchiefs, a bustle pad, nightcaps, garters, lace collars, and gloves for day and evening wear. In addition, one magazine advised, "you cannot do without less than three or four pairs of corsets;" these alone could easily cost $6.

Then there were shoes to be had (at an average cost of $1.25 a pair), purses (about another $1.00), millinery (most hats ranged from $1.99 to $3.99 each), at least one parasol (a plain one costing about $1.50), plus belts, hair decorations, and a host of other small details that made a lady of the 1890s well-dressed.

This is the second collection of patterns from the dressmaker's journal *The Voice of Fashion* that Dover Publications has offered. Besides featuring more *fabulous* dresses and street costumes, it also includes rare patterns and garments, like a tennis dress and riding habit. In addition, two evening gowns are offered, plus a rare pattern for an Empire dress. This style, harkening back to the high-waisted fashions of the late 17th and early 19th centuries, was the only fashionable alternative to the bell-shaped styles that prevailed through most of the 1890s. (Its effect was profound; by the 'teens, high-waisted dresses were the norm.)

Also included is an even more rare pattern for a house dress with a bra-like bodice decoration; this fashion appeared and disappeared within the same year. Two nightgowns are included, as well, as the three different patterns for drawers. Though we tend to think of drawers as looking essentially the same throughout the 19th century, these patterns prove that important changes in cut did occur.

Above all, notice that many of these patterns, while they might be loosely dubbed a "house" or "street" dress, were useful for a variety of purposes. With easy-to-apply changes in trimming, neckline, sleeve, or skirt, any walking dress could have served as a visiting or house dress. Evening gowns were the most elaborately trimmed, but, in general, the less lace, beading, puffing, and other decorative trim featured, the more casual the outfit was. In addition, when "misses'" dress patterns are included in this collection, it is because a simple lengthening of the skirt can make the dress equally suitable for a young woman.

## How to Use the Patterns

The patterns given in this book are scaled. There are a number of different ways to enlarge them. For either of the two methods described here, you will need a pencil, a ruler, transparent tape, and a roll of wrapping or shelf paper.

If all the patterns for a particular garment piece (such as the bodice) are in the same scale, the patterns can be enlarged by the grid method. An easy way to check whether they are in the same scale is to measure the line running along the right-hand side of the pattern. Divide this measurement into the number given at the bottom of the line. If the patterns are in the same scale, your results should be roughly the same for each piece. If the pattern pieces are to more than one scale or size, be sure to read the instructions for "The Grading Method."

As a matter of historical interest we have included the original drafting instructions for the Ladies' Costume on pages 78–85.

## The Grid Method

Begin with a major body measurement such as the waist. Next, add an appropriate amount of wearing ease (for most waistlines of this period, about ½" is appropriate). Now, in order to figure your scale, compare this total measurement with the corresponding measurement on the scaled pattern; be sure to take seam allowances and pattern pieces that represent ½ or less of the garment into consideration. If, for example, the intended wearer has a 23½" waist, plus ½" for wearing ease, and the scaled pattern's waist measurement is 2", the proper scale to use would be 1"/12". In other words, every inch on the scaled pattern would equal 12" on the full-size pattern.

Next, draw a grid on top of the scaled pattern (in this example, a 1" grid), and then draw a grid on the shelf paper (in this example, a 12" grid).

Now, transfer the lines of the scaled pattern onto the shelf paper, square by square. Whenever necessary, tape the shelf paper together to make it large enough for a full-size pattern.

## The Grading Method

When garments illustrated show pattern pieces given in more than one scale, you should use the grading method. Notice that each pattern includes sets of numbers running along all pattern lines. The numbers running along the right-hand edge of the pattern indicate length measurements; the other numbers indicate the width. Draw the pattern lines onto your paper, following all measurements carefully. It may be helpful to draw a 1" grid onto the paper before transferring pattern lines onto it, but it is not necessary. Where curves are shown, you may draw them freehand or with the aid of a French curve (available at dressmaking stores).

Once you have carefully drawn out each pattern piece according to the measurements given, you have created a "standard size" sloper for the garment. This, by modern standards, is quite small and will need to be graded to fit the modern figure. If you are unfamiliar with the practice of grading patterns, follow the instructions given below or consult a dressmaking book at your local library.

**To Adjust Width:** Changes will almost certainly need to be made in the width of your pattern. To determine how much change is necessary, subtract your actual measurements (including wearing ease and seam allowances) from the corresponding pattern measurements. For example, if your waist measurement is 25½" and the pattern measurement is 19", you need to enlarge your pattern by 6½" in the waist area. Now, divide the amount you must enlarge the pattern (in our example 6½") by the number of bodice pattern pieces (for our example, say 4). This will tell you how much to enlarge each pattern piece (in our example, 1⅝"). Slash the pattern pieces as illustrated in *Fig. 1*, and spread in a triangular fashion. Place a piece of paper behind the slashed section and tape it into place.

To take in the pattern, make a tuck in the pattern as shown in *Fig. 1* and redraw the cutting and seam lines.

**To Adjust Length:** If your garment needs adjustment in length, either fold it (if too long) or slash and spread it (if too short) (*Fig. 2*).

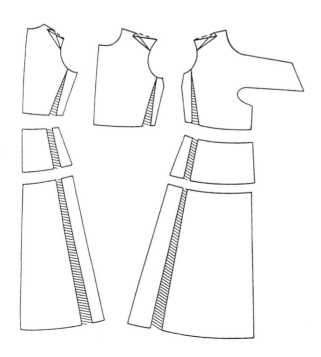

*Fig. 1.* To adjust width.

*Fig. 2.* To adjust length.

**Remember:**

• In most cases, allowances for closures (hooks and eyes, buttons, plackets) and facings are not included on the pattern and must be added before cutting out the pattern in fabric.

• Carefully label all pattern pieces and transfer any construction markings to the full-size pattern.

• If a corset and other undergarments are to be worn, the body measurements should be taken in these undergarments.

• It may be necessary to use different scales for different parts of each garment even if the pattern pieces for each part are in the same scale. For instance, the bodice may require a larger scale than the skirt, especially if a corset will not be worn beneath the finished garment.

• The length of most skirt patterns is not proportional. Regulate the length of skirts by personal length measurements.

• Always remember to add wearing ease to your body measurements before figuring the scale on which to enlarge your pattern. If you make your pattern to your exact measurements, the resulting garment will be skin tight, and will probably rip with every movement. Ease must be added to make clothes fit comfortably. The typical 1890s waistline had about ½" to 1" ease, and the average snug-fitting bustline had about 2½" of ease.

• Because there is no "standard" body, testing and perfecting the pattern in muslin before cutting out the fashion fabric is advised.

TO TAKE MEASURES. Great care should be taken in getting measures. (See illustration below.)

TAKE BUST MEASURE with the tape measure straight around the largest part of the bust, as shown below, high up under the arms; take a snug, close measure neither too tight nor too loose.

TAKE MEASURE AROUND THE WAIST as tight as the dress is to be worn.

TAKE LENGTH OF WAIST from the large joint where neck and body join, down to the waist. Care must be taken to get this measure.

SLEEVE MEASURE is taken from the center of back to wrist joint, with arm raised and elbow bent.

IN CUTTING a garment look carefully at the drafts being copied; use numbers and curves as shown in draft.

THE ARROWS are used for two purposes—one to show which way to turn the curve, the other the number of points to be connected with the curve.

THE CURVE should always be turned with the largest part in the direction in which the arrow points.

When the arrow is placed *between* two lines it shows that only two points are to be connected.

When the arrow is placed upon a *cross line* it shows that three points must be connected with the curve, that the point by the arrow is the middle one, and the points nearest on each side must be connected with the curve at the same time with larger part of the curve turned in the direction the arrow points.

The letter A in corner of draft is the starting point in making draft.

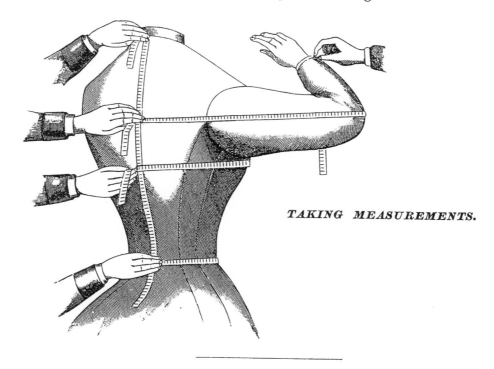

*TAKING MEASUREMENTS.*

---

## DIRECTIONS FOR BASTING.

FIRST:—Smooth, even tracing is very necessary. Place the pattern smooth on lining crosswise. Trace each line carefully. Cut out the lining same as pattern. Place the lining straight on the goods, the nap, if any, running down. Pin the lining at the waist line. Full the lining (from ¼ to ½ inch) each side of the waist line, from 1½ inches below the waist line to 2½ inches above, the greatest fullness coming at the waist line; this shortens the lining, but when boned it will be stretched to place. Leave the lining easy each way, from top of darts to shoulders, and one-fourth of an inch full at center of shoulder line. Never backstitch in basting or draw the thread tight.

In joining the different parts together, care must be taken, as smooth, even basting is necessary. Pass the needle exactly through the traced seam lines on both sides of the seam, as many garments are ruined by careless basting.

In joining the back and side-back, hold the side-back to you, thus you will baste one up and the other down. It is a good idea to pin these pieces before basting. If the shoulder blades are prominent, hold the back piece a little full where the shoulder blades strike to within 1½ inches of arms-eye. In basting the shoulders, hold the back to you. Baste evenly for one inch, then stretch the front shoulder to match the back, for the back is always cut longer.

1

# MISSES' WRAPPER.
## Summer 1893

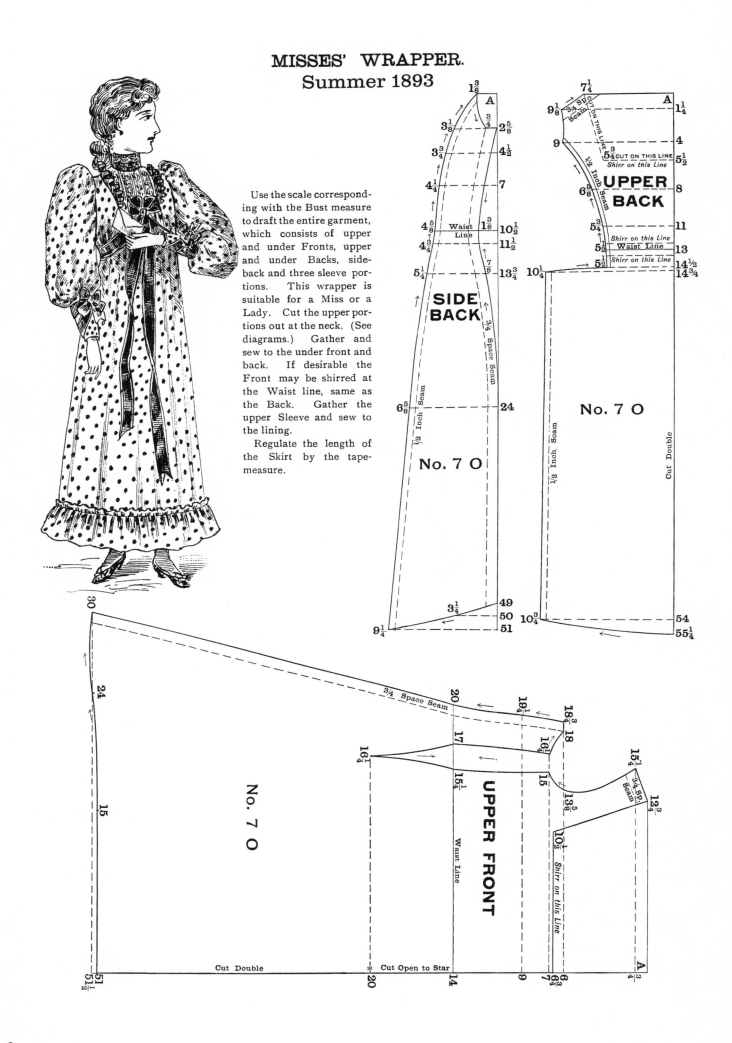

Use the scale corresponding with the Bust measure to draft the entire garment, which consists of upper and under Fronts, upper and under Backs, side-back and three sleeve portions. This wrapper is suitable for a Miss or a Lady. Cut the upper portions out at the neck. (See diagrams.) Gather and sew to the under front and back. If desirable the Front may be shirred at the Waist line, same as the Back. Gather the upper Sleeve and sew to the lining.

Regulate the length of the Skirt by the tape-measure.

SIDE BACK

No. 7 O

UPPER BACK

No. 7 O

Cut Double

UPPER FRONT

No. 7 O

Waist Line

Cut Double

Cut Open to Star

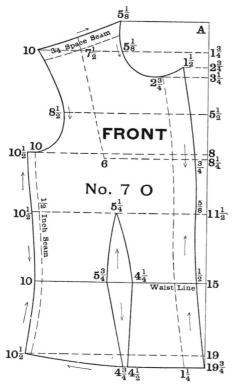

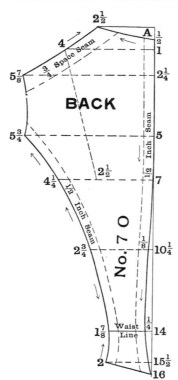

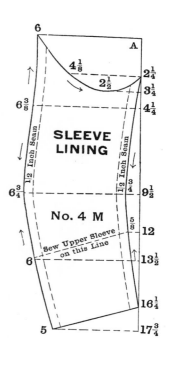

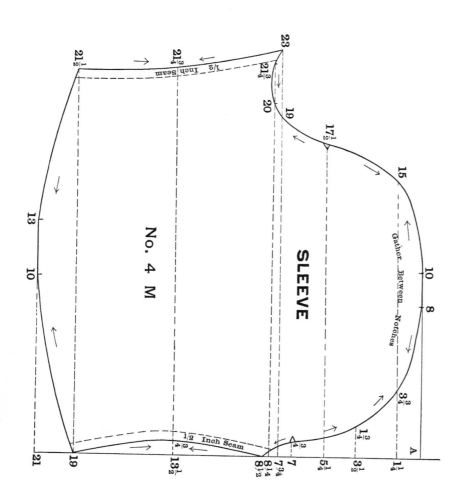

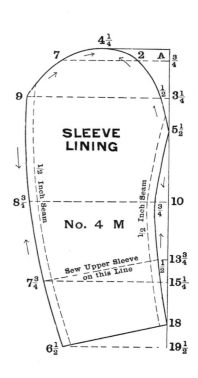

# LADIES' TEA GOWN.
## Spring 1893

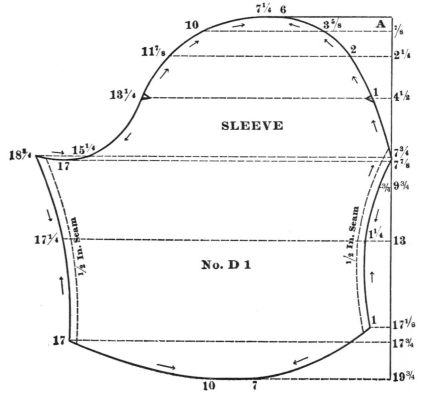

**UPPER FRONT**

No. B 11

Join under front to this Line.

Sew under front in this Dart

WAIST

4¼ LINE

**SLEEVE**

No. D 1

Use scale corresponding with the Bust measure to draft the entire garment, which consists of three front portions, Back and Side-back, Sleeve and Cuff.

The shirring is made of lace or soft silk. Join the different portions as indicated on the cuts. Any style of trimming may be used.

Regulate the length by the tape-measure.

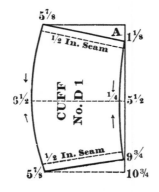

**CUFF No. D 1**

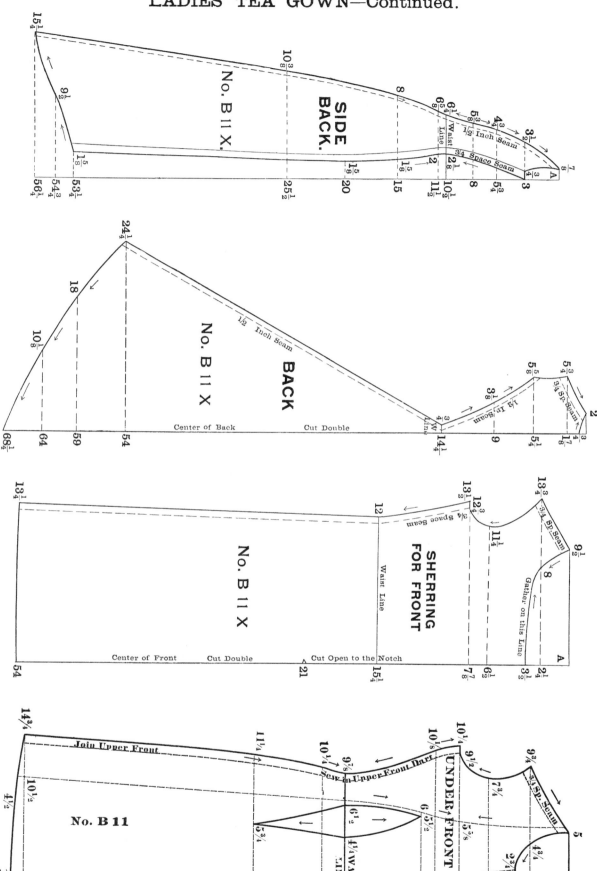

## LADIES' DRAWERS.
### Fall 1890

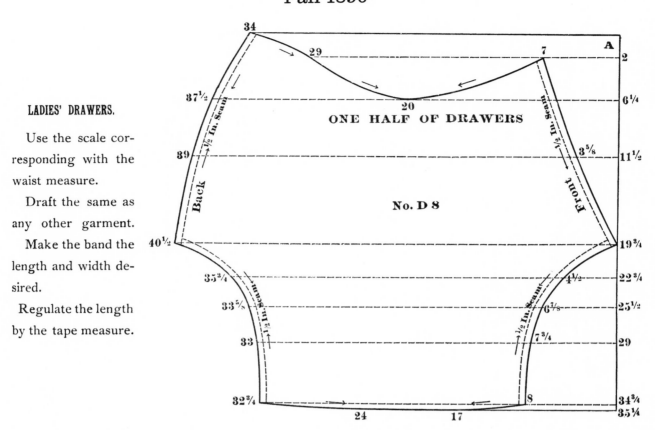

**LADIES' DRAWERS.**

Use the scale corresponding with the waist measure.

Draft the same as any other garment.

Make the band the length and width desired.

Regulate the length by the tape measure.

## LADIES' DRAWERS.
### Spring 1893

Use the scale corresponding with the Waist measure to draft the entire garment, which consists of one-half of the drawers and band.

Make allowance for tucks.   Regulate by the tape measure.

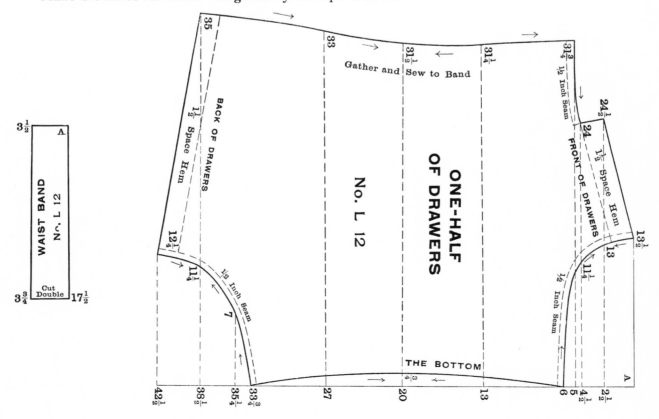

Select the scale corresponding with the waist measure.

It is in two pieces: One-half of the drawers and one-half of the band. These can be closed or left open.

Gather the extra fullness at the top and sew to the band.

Make all allowances for tucks.

Regulate the length by the tape line.

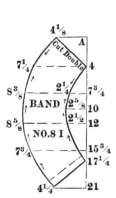

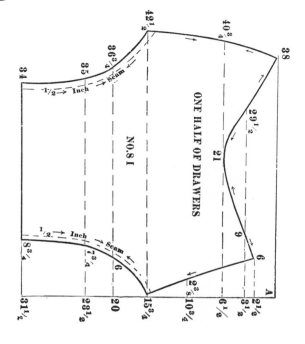

# LADIES' STREET COSTUME.
## Fall 1890

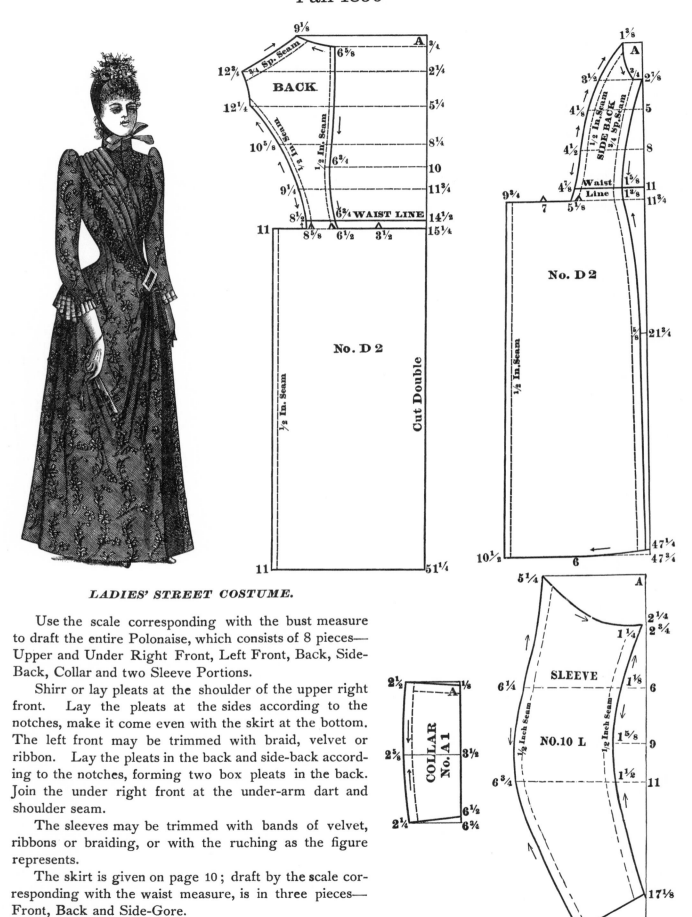

### LADIES' STREET COSTUME.

Use the scale corresponding with the bust measure to draft the entire Polonaise, which consists of 8 pieces—Upper and Under Right Front, Left Front, Back, Side-Back, Collar and two Sleeve Portions.

Shirr or lay pleats at the shoulder of the upper right front. Lay the pleats at the sides according to the notches, make it come even with the skirt at the bottom. The left front may be trimmed with braid, velvet or ribbon. Lay the pleats in the back and side-back according to the notches, forming two box pleats in the back. Join the under right front at the under-arm dart and shoulder seam.

The sleeves may be trimmed with bands of velvet, ribbons or braiding, or with the ruching as the figure represents.

The skirt is given on page 10; draft by the scale corresponding with the waist measure, is in three pieces—Front, Back and Side-Gore.

Regulate the length by the tape measure.

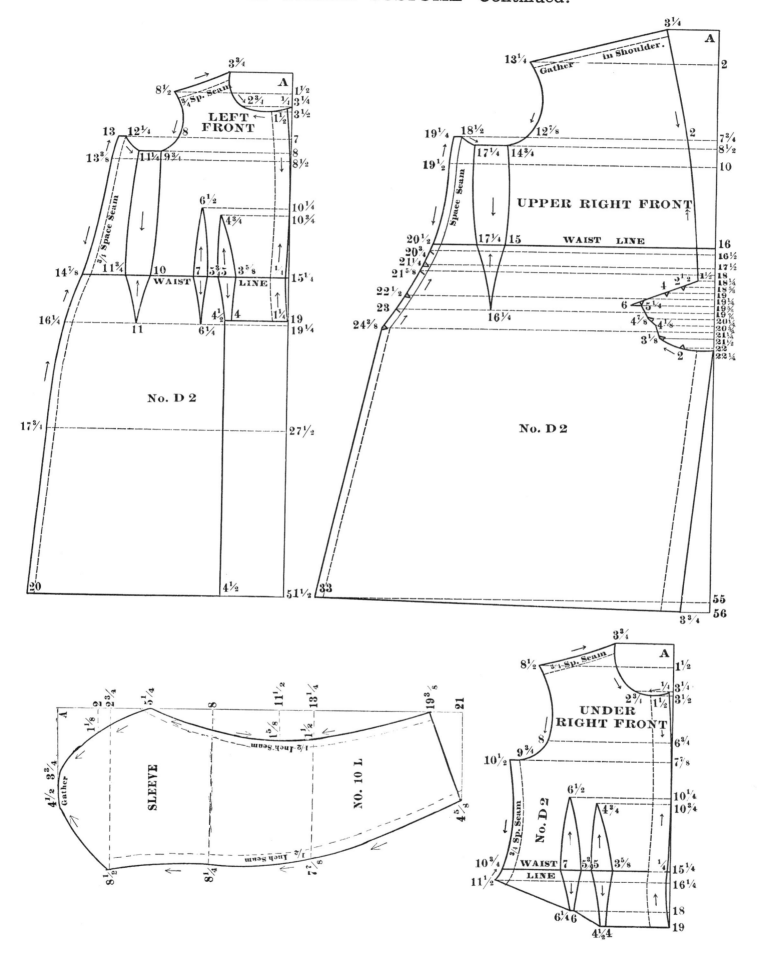

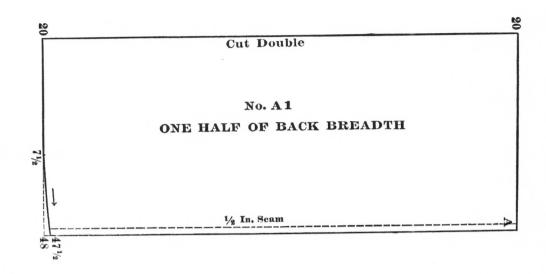

No. A 1
ONE HALF OF BACK BREADTH

Cut Double

½ In. Seam

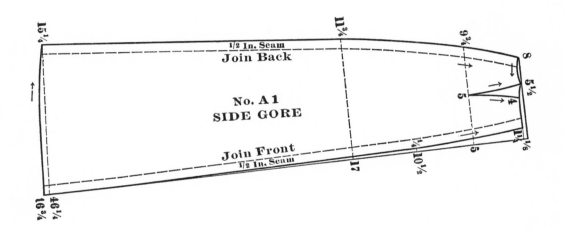

No. A 1
SIDE GORE

½ In. Seam
Join Back

Join Front
½ In. Seam

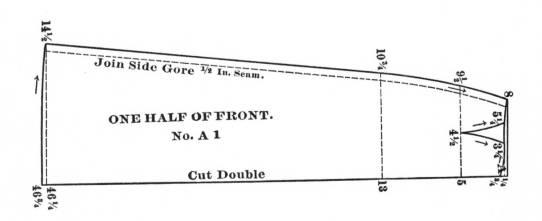

Join Side Gore ½ In. Seam.

ONE HALF OF FRONT.
No. A 1

Cut Double

# YOUNG MISSES' STREET COSTUME.
## Fall 1890

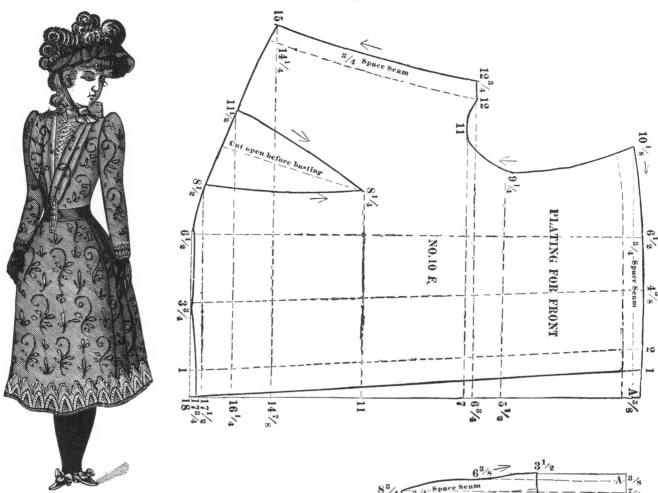

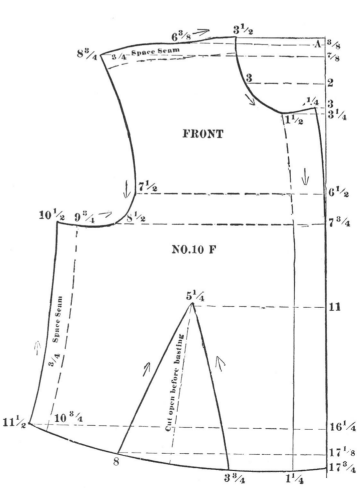

**YOUNG MISSES' STREET COSTUME.**

Use the scale corresponding with the bust measure to draft the entire waist and sleeves, which consists of Upper and Under Fronts and Backs, Side Back and two Sleeve portions

Draft this the same as all others.

Lay pleats in the front and back as represented.

Gather the sleeves at the top to fit the armseye.

Draft the skirt by the scale corresponding with the waist measure.

Trim to suit.

Regulate the length by the tape measure.

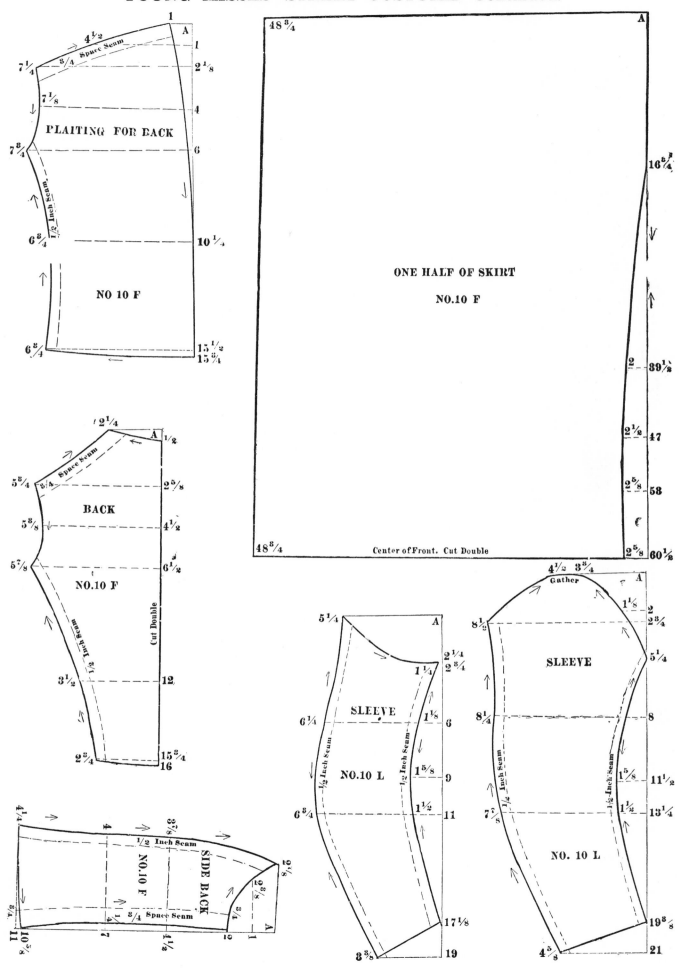

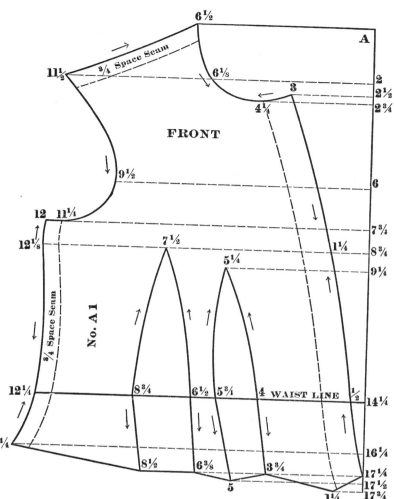

*STREET COSTUME.*

Use the scale corresponding with the bust meas-ure to draft the entire waist, which consists of Up-per and Under Fronts, Back, Side Back, Under Arm-gore, Collar, and Sleeve.

Baste the side form on to the back as far down as the seam line is marked, and from there down to the bottom, lap the side form over the back; fin-ish with small buttons, set close together, on each side of the back. Face the upper front as far back as the dotted line, and turn back for a rolling collar, extending to the bottom of the garment. Take up the dart, cut out and press the seam open, Join to the under arm-gore; also join the under front or vest to the under arm-gore.

The diagrams for the drapery are given on page 15. Draft by the scale corresponding with the waist measure. It consists of two pieces: Front and Back. Lay the back in two double box pleats. Lay the pleats in the front according to the notches; make it even with the skirt. Cut the foundation skirt from any of the plain skirt patterns. Regulate to suit.

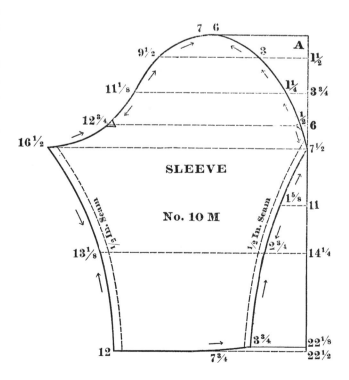

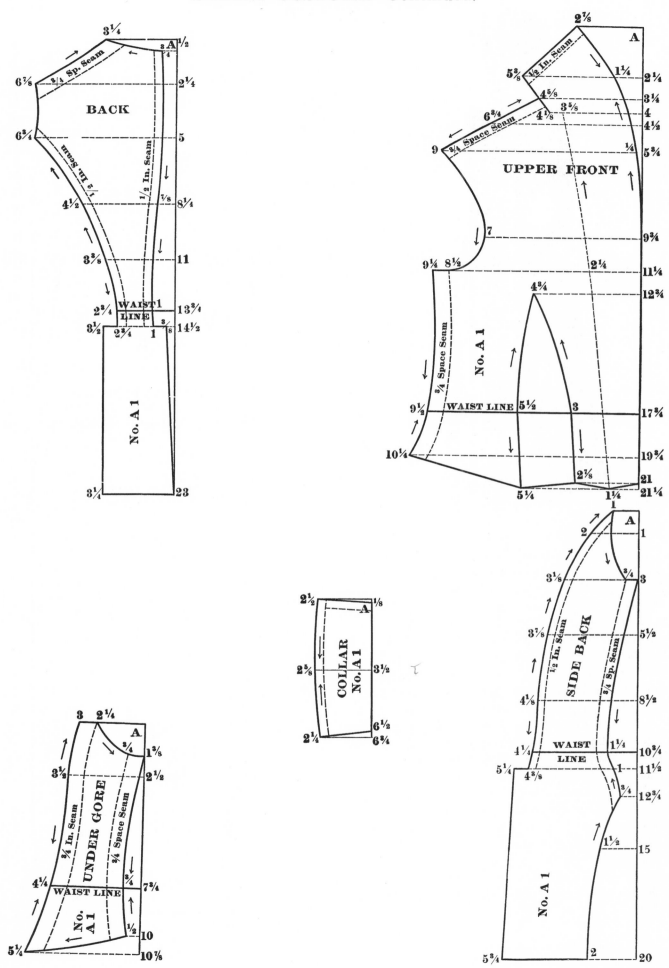

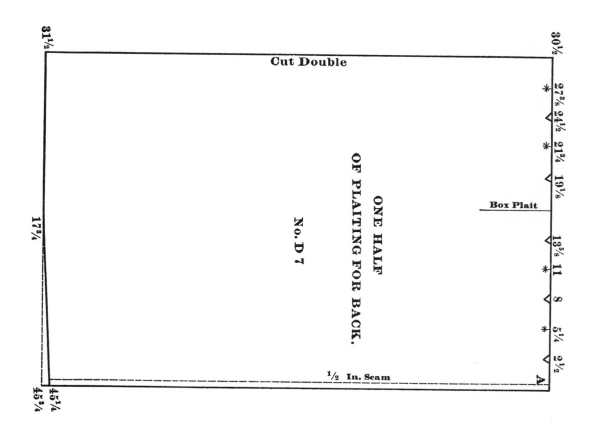

**Cut Double**

ONE HALF
OF PLAITING FOR BACK.

No. D 7

Box Plait

30½   27⅞ *   24½   21¾ *   19⅛   13⅝   11 *   8   5¼ *   2½

31½   17¾   45¾   45¼

½ In. Seam   A

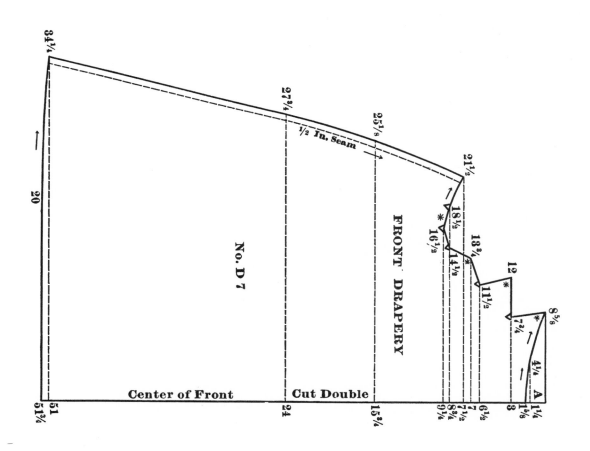

No. D 7

FRONT DRAPERY

Center of Front   Cut Double

½ In. Seam

34¼   27¾   25⅛   21½   18½ *   16½   14½   13¾ *   12 *   11½   8⅝ *   7¾   4¼   A 1¼

20   51   51¾   24   15¾   9¼   8¾   7½   7   6½   3   1⅝

# LADIES' STREET COSTUME.
## Winter 1890-91

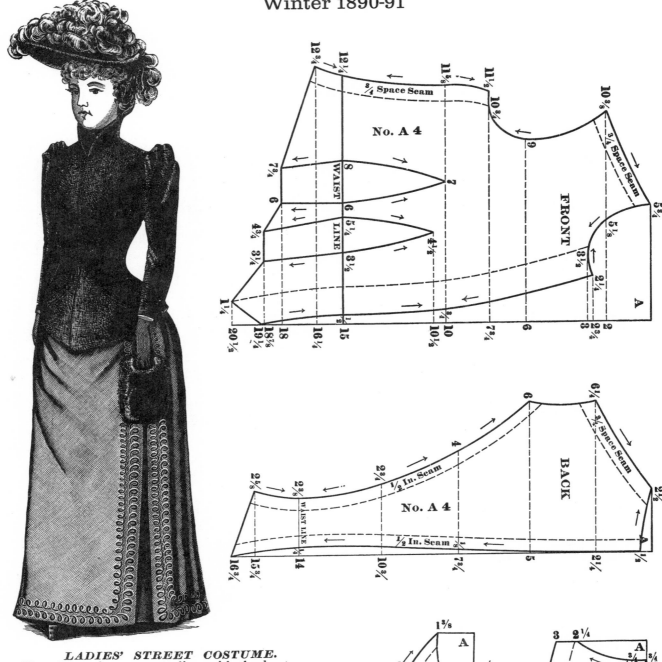

### LADIES' STREET COSTUME.

Use the scale corresponding with the bust measure to draft the basque, which consists of front-back, side-back and under-arm-gore. Braid the waist down the front and the sleeves same as the skirt. The jacket is given on page 17. Draft by bust measure; it consists of front-back, side-back, under-arm-gore, standing and medici collars, and two sleeve portions. Sew the medici collar on the dotted line, close the front with large patent hooks, make the garment as long as desirable.

The drapery is given on page 18. Draft with scale corresponding with the waist measure; is in two pieces, front and back; lay the pleats in the front according to the notches, gather or pleat the back. The diagrams for the foundation skirt are given on page 19. Draft by waist measure. It consists of front, back and side-gore. Regulate the length of the entire garment by the tape measure.

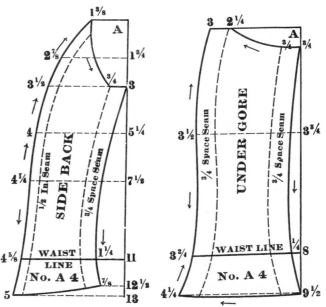

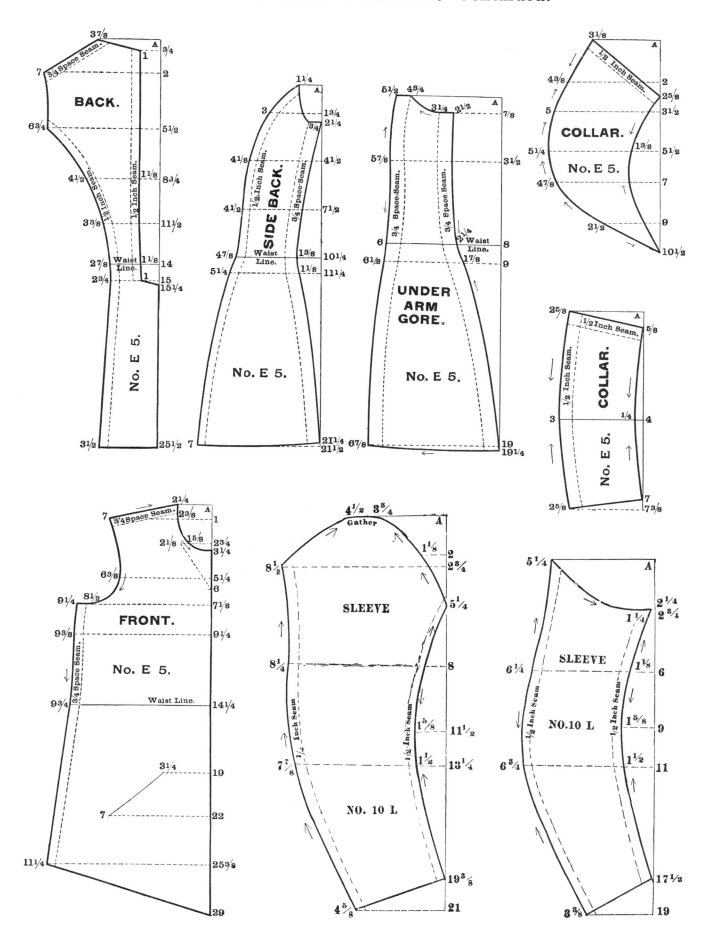

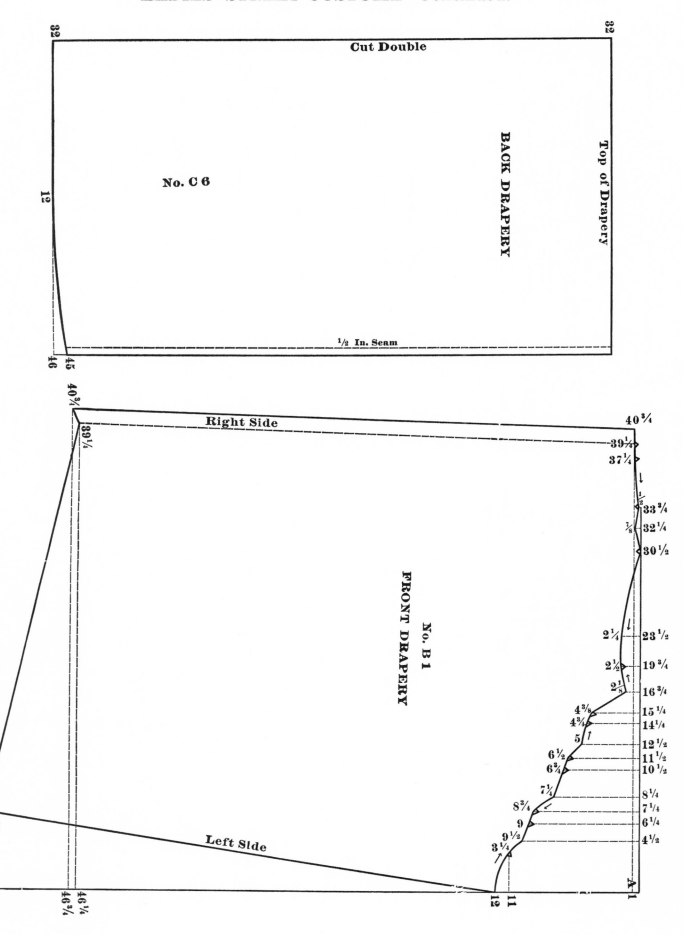

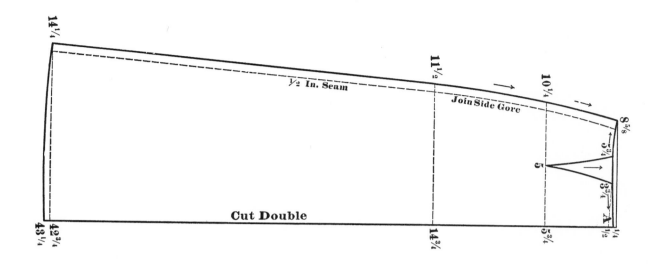

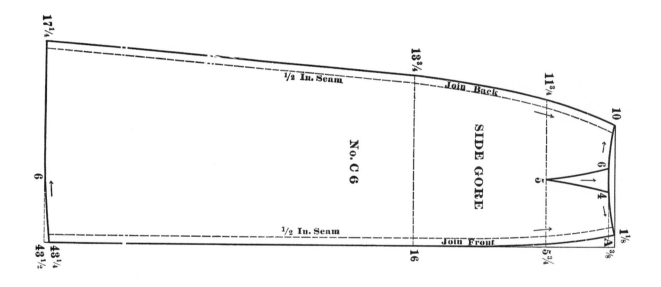

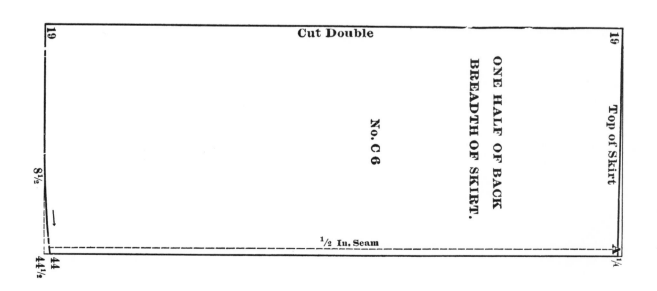

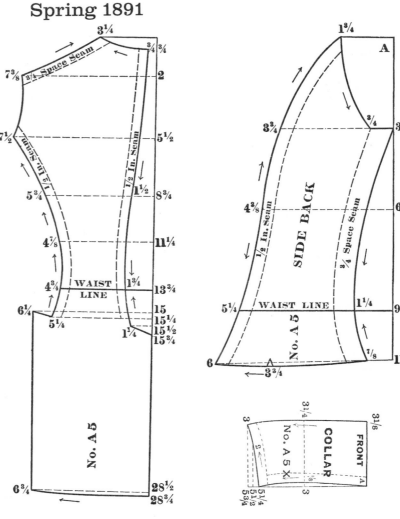

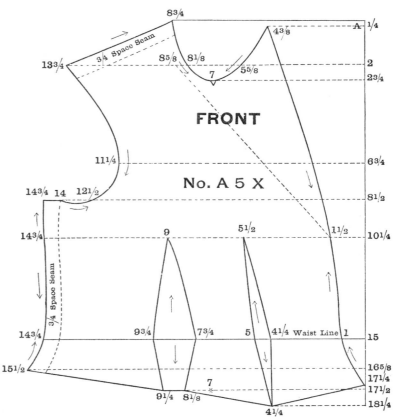

Use the scale corresponding with the bust measure to draft the jacket, which consists of front and skirt, back, side back, collar, pocket lap and two sleeve portions. Draft this the same as all other garments. Baste the front and side back together, take up the darts, then baste the skirt on; connect the notches. Bring the front of the collar to the notch in front. Gather or pleat the sleeves very full on the top. Make the jacket to match the suit or of any suitable material.

The drapery is drafted by the waist measure. The diagrams are given on pages 21 and 22. Lay the pleats according to the notches. Face the bottom with silk or any suitable material. Use any waist given in this issue or any other. The jacket may be trimmed to correspond with the skirt, that is the rolling collar, sleeves and pocket laps.

Regulate the length of the entire garment with the tape measure.

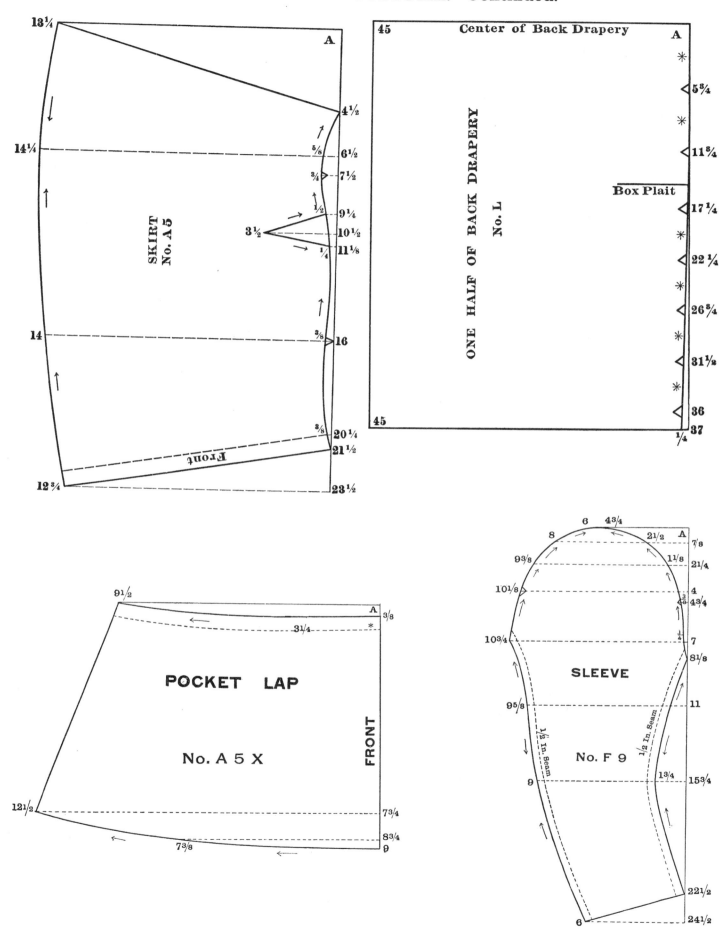

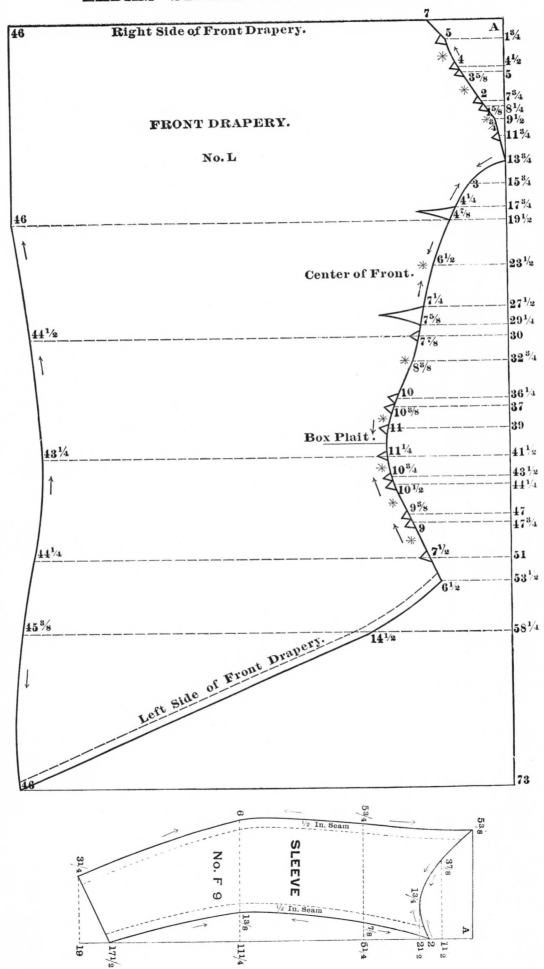

**Right Side of Front Drapery.**

46

**FRONT DRAPERY.**

**No. L**

A

7

5 — 1¾

4 — 4½

3⅝ — 5

2 — 7¾

5⅝ — 8¼

8 — 9½

¾ — 11¾

— 13¾

46

**Center of Front.**

3 — 15¾

4¼ — 17¾

4⅞ — 19½

6½ — 23½

7¼ — 27½

7⅝ — 29¼

7⅞ — 30

44½

8⅜ — 32¾

10 — 36¼

10⅜ — 37

**Box Plait.**

11 — 39

11¼ — 41½

43¼

10¾ — 43½

10½ — 44¼

9⅜ — 47

9 — 47¾

44¼

7½ — 51

6½ — 53½

45⅜

14½ — 58¼

**Left Side of Front Drapery.**

46

73

6

5¾

5⅜

½ In. Seam

**SLEEVE**

**No. F 9**

3¾

3⅞

1¾

7⅞

½ In. Seam

13⅜

5¼

19

17½

11¼

5¼

A

2

2½

2

1½

# YOUNG MISSES' STREET COSTUME.
## Spring 1891

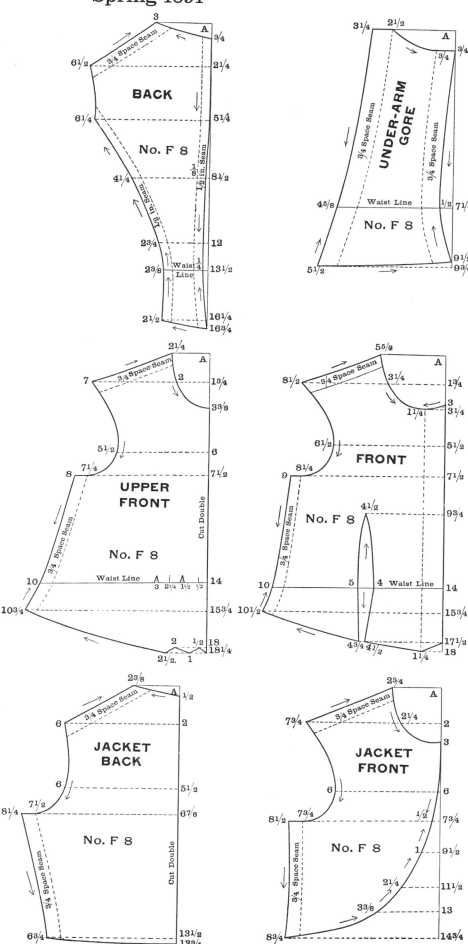

Use the scale corresponding with the bust measure to draft waist and jacket—the waist consists of upper and under front, back, side back, under-arm-gore and girdle. Lay pleats on the upper front according to the notches, close with hooks and eyes on the shoulder and under the arms. The jacket may be omitted if desirable.

The skirt and drapery is drafted by the waist measure. The skirt is in three pieces—front, back breadth and side-gore. The drapery is in one piece. Lay the pleats according to the notches. Make a box pleat over the hip and two in the back. Trim to suit. Regulate the length by the tape measure.

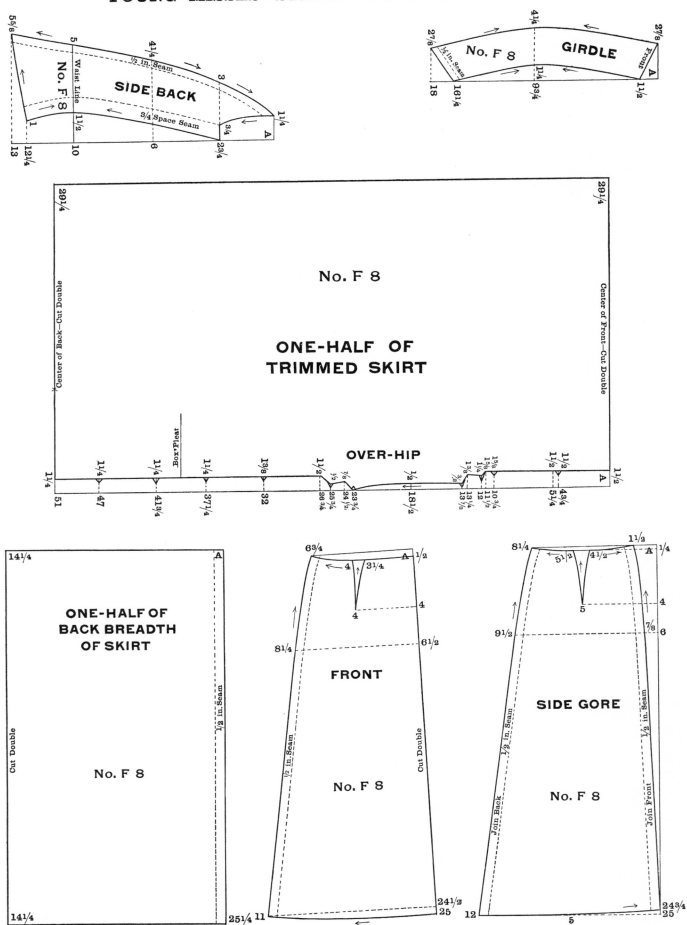

# LADIES' STREET COSTUME
## Spring 1893

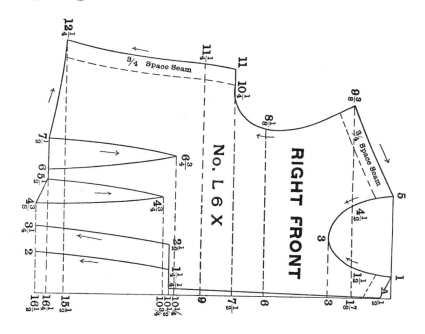

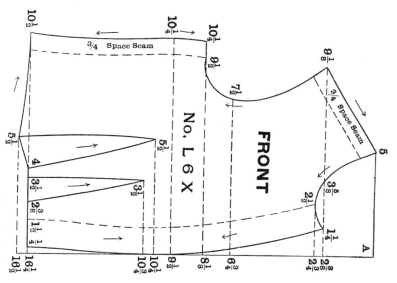

Use the scale corresponding with the Bust measure to draft the entire waist, which consists of two Fronts, Back, Collar and three sleeve portions. The Back is seamless. Be sure and cut but one of each fronts, as one is for the right side and the other is for the left. Gather the upper part of the sleeve at the bottom, sew it to the under sleeve, gather it through the center or on the dotted line; draw it up to fit the under sleeve, then gather the top; also gather the top of the under sleeve. The sleeve lining on page 28 may be used instead for the under sleeve, if desired, as it will not require so much material.

The Skirt is given on pages 26 and 27. Draft by the waist measure; it is in four pieces—two Fronts, Back and Side Gore. Join the upper front to to the back. The under front and side-gore may be made of a contrasting material, with good results.

Regulate the length by the tape measure.

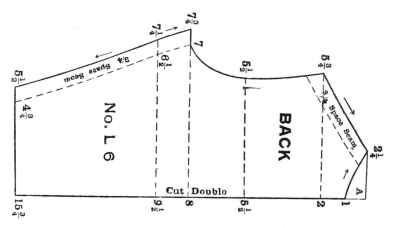

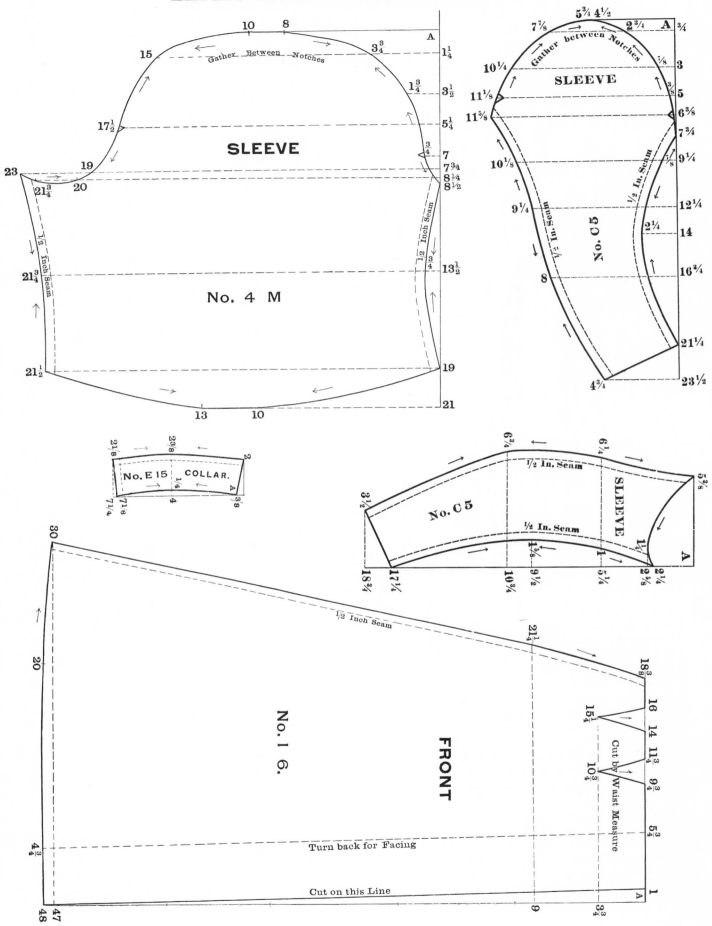

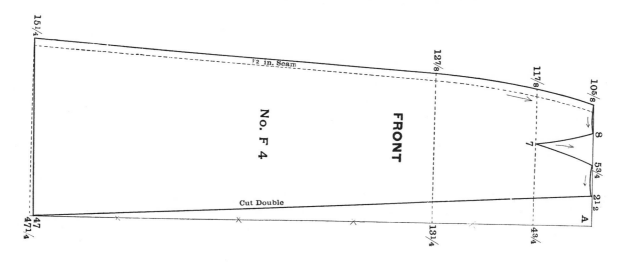

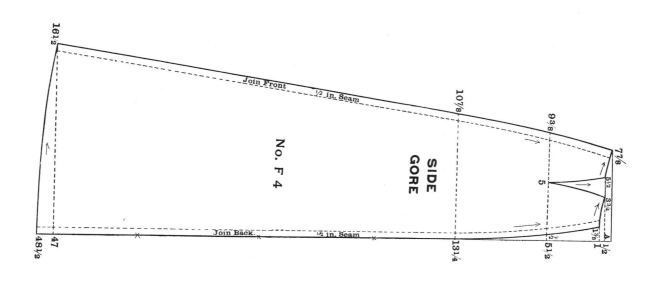

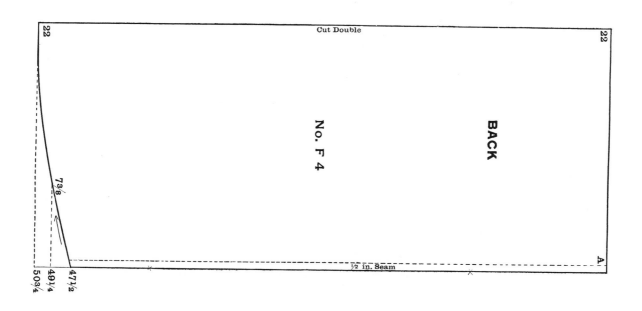

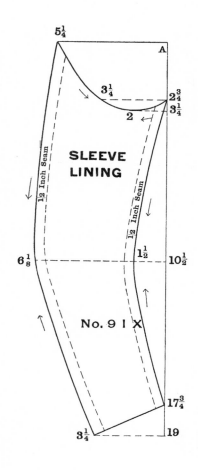

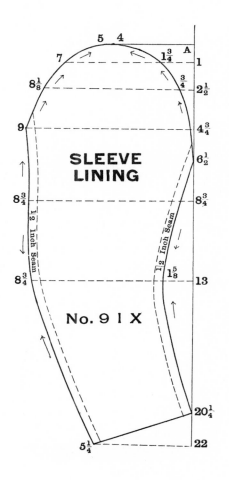

# LADIES' STREET COSTUME.
## Spring 1893

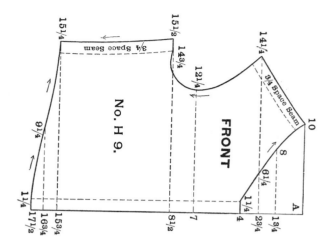

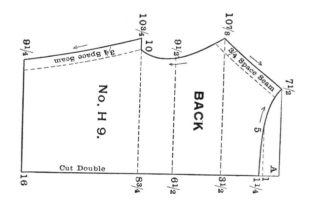

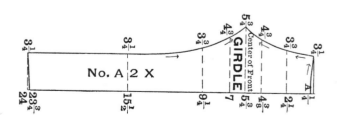

*LADIES' STREET COSTUME.*

Use the scale corresponding with the Bust measure to draft the Waist, Jacket and Sleeves. The waist is in six pieces, namely: Front, Back, Girdle, Collar and two Sleeve portions. Gather at the neck and waist; cut the back double.

The Jacket is given on page 30. The back is cut double, round it in the center. This is very pretty made of black velvet with the large full sleeve puff given on page 26, omitting the shirring through the center if made of the velvet. Trim it all around and up the back with fancy tinsel or gimp; trim around the arm's eye also. The effect is very pretty.

The skirt is given on page 31. Draft by the waist measure. This is a one piece skirt. Gather it all all around, putting most of the fulness in the center of the back. Trim the bottom to suit.

Regulate the length by the tape-measure.

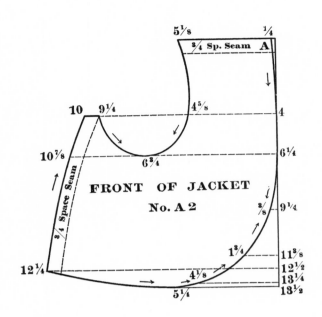

FRONT OF JACKET
No. A 2

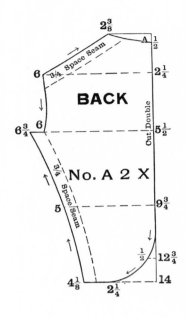

BACK

No. A 2 X

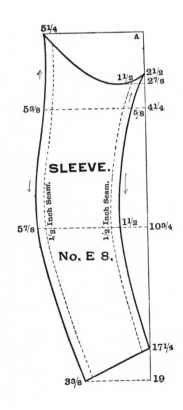

SLEEVE.

No. E 8.

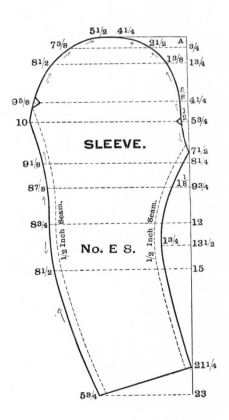

SLEEVE.

No. E 8.

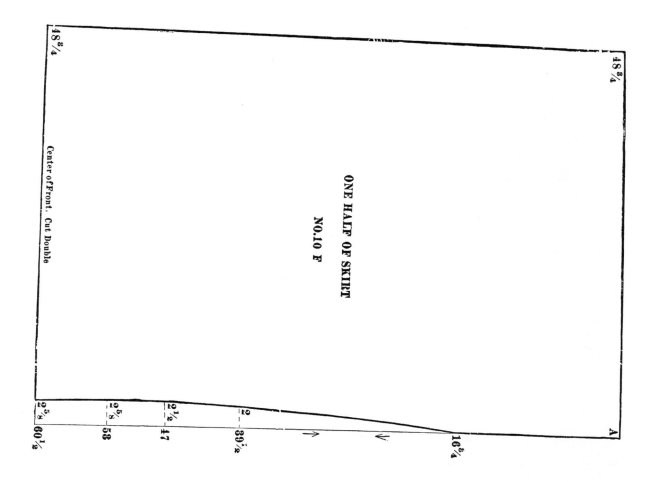

ONE HALF OF SKIRT
NO. 10 F

Center of Front. Cut Double

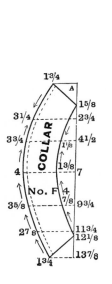

COLLAR

No. F 4

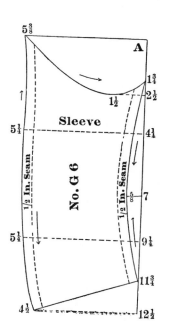

Sleeve

No. G 6

½ In. Seam

½ In. Seam

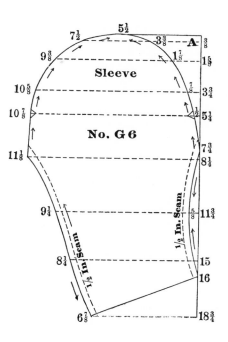

Sleeve

No. G 6

½ In. Seam

½ In. Seam

# LADIES' STREET COSTUME.
## Spring 1893

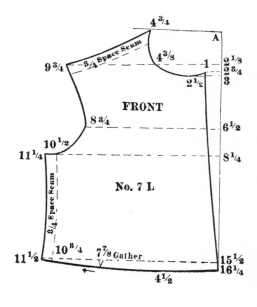

Use the scale corresponding with the Bust measure to draft the entire Waist, Jacket and Sleeves.

The Waist consists of Front, Back, Top of Sleeve, Sleeve Band, Puff and Cuff. Gather the waist between the notches and sew to a belt. Fasten on the left side invisibly.

The Jacket is cut in one piece. This gives the pointed front which may be rounded off if preferred, or the point may be cut shorter. Turn back on the dotted line for revers. The diagrams for Jacket, Cuff and Puff are given on Page 34.

The Skirt is given on Page 33 Draft by waist measure, this gives the six gores and also the fullness, so much desired at present. Put the different parts together according to the stars, gather the extra fullness in at the waist. Regulate the length to suit.

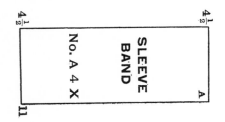

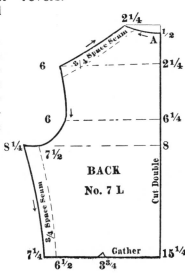

# LADIES' STREET COSTUME—Continued.

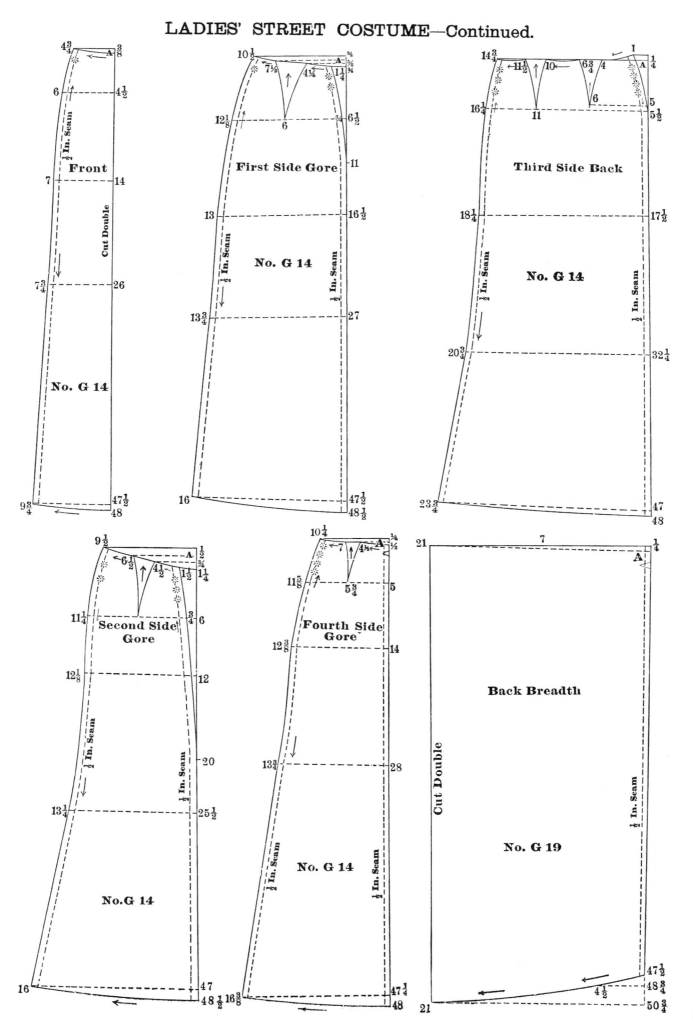

**Front** — No. G 14 — Cut Double — ½ In. Seam

**First Side Gore** — No. G 14 — ½ In. Seam

**Third Side Back** — No. G 14 — ½ In. Seam

**Second Side Gore** — No. G 14 — ½ In. Seam

**Fourth Side Gore** — No. G 14 — ½ In. Seam

**Back Breadth** — No. G 19 — Cut Double — ½ In. Seam

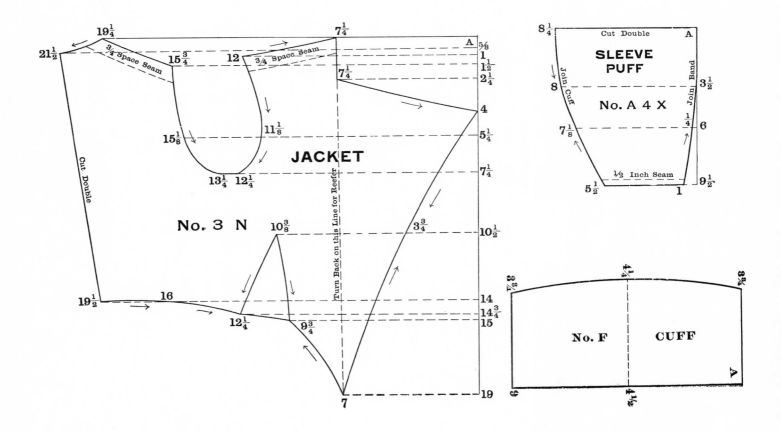

# LADIES' STREET COSTUME.
## Summer 1893

Use the scale corresponding with the Bust Measure to draft the Waist, Sleeves and Cape. The Waist consists of front, back, side-back, two under arm gores, two sleeve portions and collar. This is suitable for a medium form. The bottom may be shaped to suit the wearer. The Cape is in one piece. The diagram is given on page 37. Line with silk; trim with velvet satin bands, or folds.

The Skirt is drafted by the Waist Measure. It is in one piece. This is a very full skirt, some call it the fluted lamp shade. It looks best trimmed with flat bands or milliner folds, or scant ruffles. Make it clear the floor all around. Regulate the length by the tape-measure.

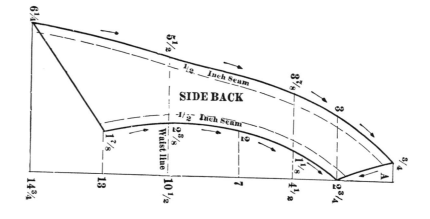

**FRONT** diagram with measurements including: $5\frac{1}{4}$, A, $9\frac{7}{8}$, $\frac{3}{4}$ Space Seam, $4\frac{3}{4}$, $1\frac{7}{8}$, $9\frac{1}{8}$, $3\frac{1}{4}$, $2\frac{1}{4}$, $3\frac{3}{8}$, Turn away for a V, $8\frac{1}{2}$, $6\frac{1}{2}$, $10\frac{3}{8}$, $9\frac{7}{8}$, $1\frac{1}{2}$, $8\frac{1}{2}$, $10\frac{1}{4}$, $6\frac{1}{2}$, $4\frac{1}{2}$, $2\frac{1}{4}$, $11\frac{1}{4}$, $1\frac{1}{4}$, $11\frac{7}{8}$, $\frac{1}{2}$ Inch Seam, Cut open before basting, $10\frac{1}{4}$, $7\frac{1}{4}$, $5\frac{1}{2}$, $4\frac{5}{8}$, $3\frac{1}{4}$, 2, 1, $16\frac{1}{2}$, Waist line, 11, $19\frac{3}{8}$, $6\frac{1}{2}$, $5\frac{1}{4}$, $21\frac{1}{4}$, 4, 3, $21\frac{3}{4}$, 1, $22\frac{3}{4}$

**COLLAR NO.10 L** diagram with measurements: $2\frac{5}{8}$, $\frac{3}{8}$, A, $2\frac{5}{8}$, $3\frac{8}{8}$, 3, 2, $6\frac{1}{8}$, $6\frac{3}{4}$

**SIDE BACK** diagram with measurements: $6\frac{1}{4}$, $5\frac{1}{2}$, $\frac{1}{2}$ Inch Seam, $3\frac{7}{8}$, 3, $\frac{1}{2}$ Inch Seam, $1\frac{7}{8}$, Waist line, $2\frac{3}{8}$, 2, $1\frac{1}{8}$, A, $\frac{3}{4}$, $14\frac{3}{4}$, 13, $10\frac{1}{2}$, 7, $4\frac{1}{2}$, $2\frac{3}{4}$

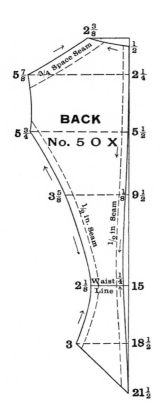

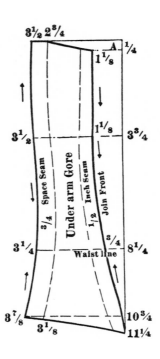

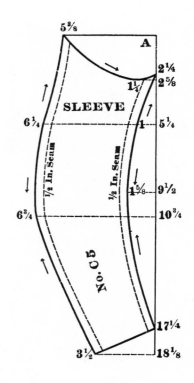

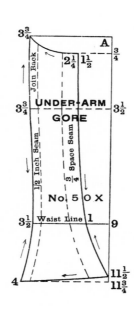

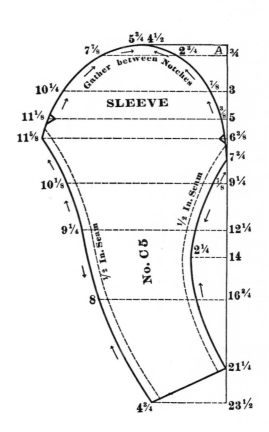

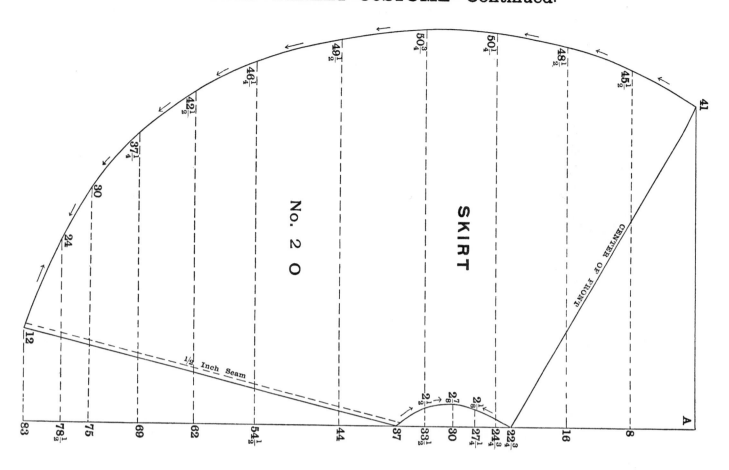

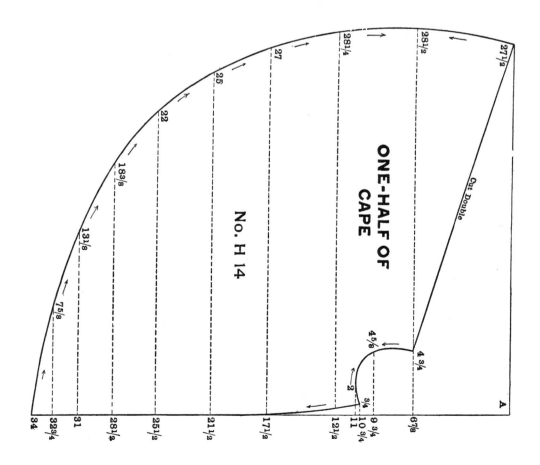

# LADIES' STREET COSTUME.
## Summer 1893

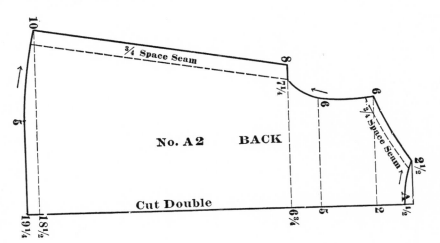

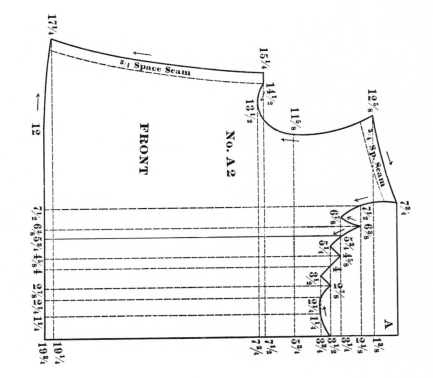

Use the scale corresponding with the Bust Measure to draft the entire Waist and Sleeves.

The Blouse Waist consists of Front, Back, Sleeve, Cuff and Collar. Tuck the Front, hem the bottom and wear under the Skirt.

The Jacket is in two pieces, Front and Back. Make of velvet, trim with embroidery.

The Skirt is drafted by the Waist Measure; is in one piece. Gather all around, bringing most of the fullness in the center of the back. Trim to suit, either with velvet or satin.

Regulate the length by the tape-measure.

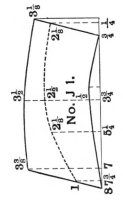

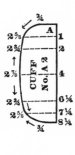

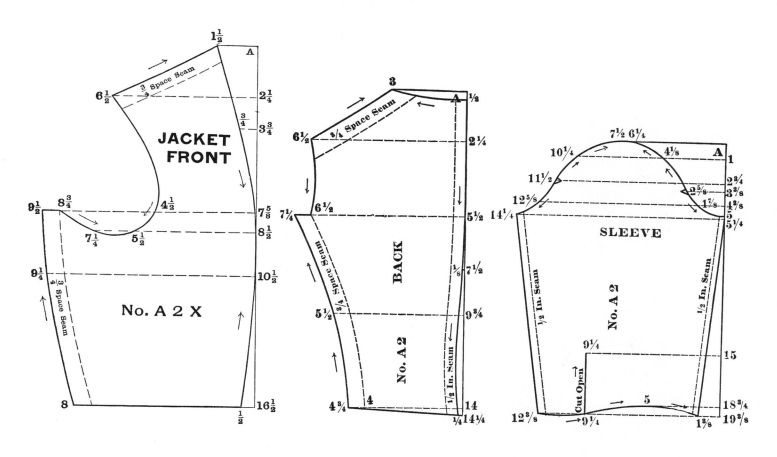

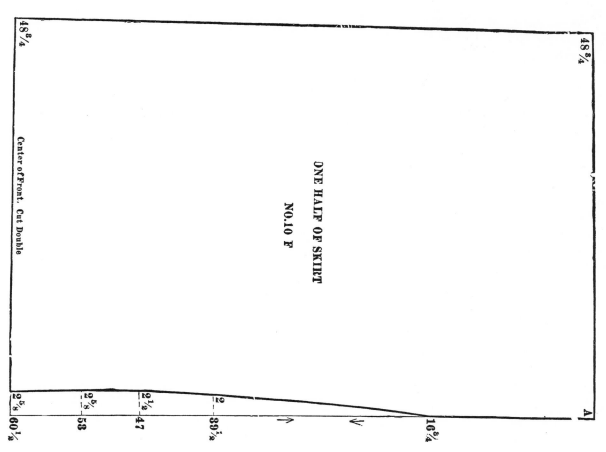

# LADIES' STREET COSTUME.
## Summer 1893

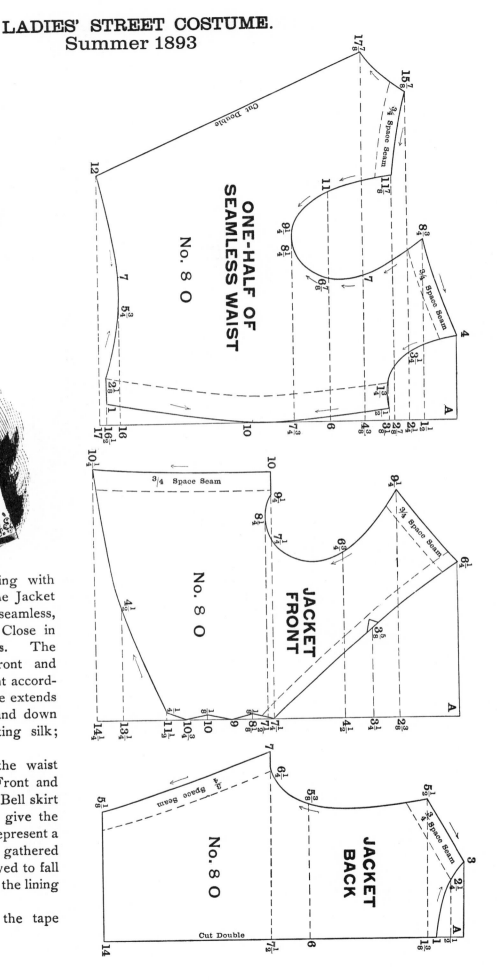

**ONE-HALF OF SEAMLESS WAIST**
No. 80

**JACKET FRONT**
No. 80

**JACKET BACK**
No. 80

Use the scale corresponding with the Bust Measure to draft the Jacket and Waist. The waist is the seamless, except the shoulder seams. Close in front with hooks and eyes. The Jacket is in two pieces—Front and Back. Lay the pleats in front according to the notches; the bretelle extends across the back of the neck and down the front line with contrasting silk; gather on the dotted line.

The Skirt is drafted by the waist measure; is in two pieces, Front and Back breadth. This is the Bell skirt with a back breadth set in to give the required fullness. Trim to represent a double skirt. The sleeve is gathered all around the top and allowed to fall down over the arms. Tack to the lining to keep in place.

Regulate the length by the tape measure.

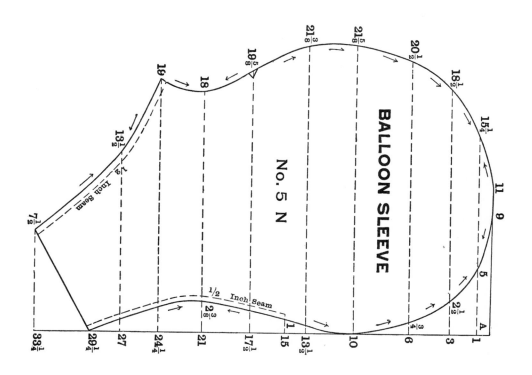

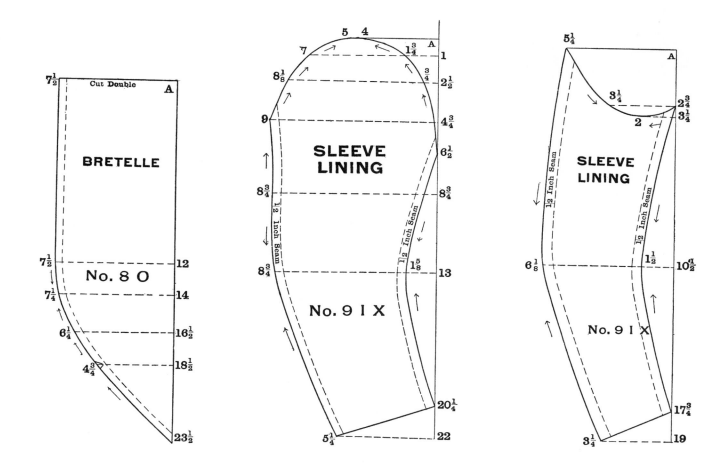

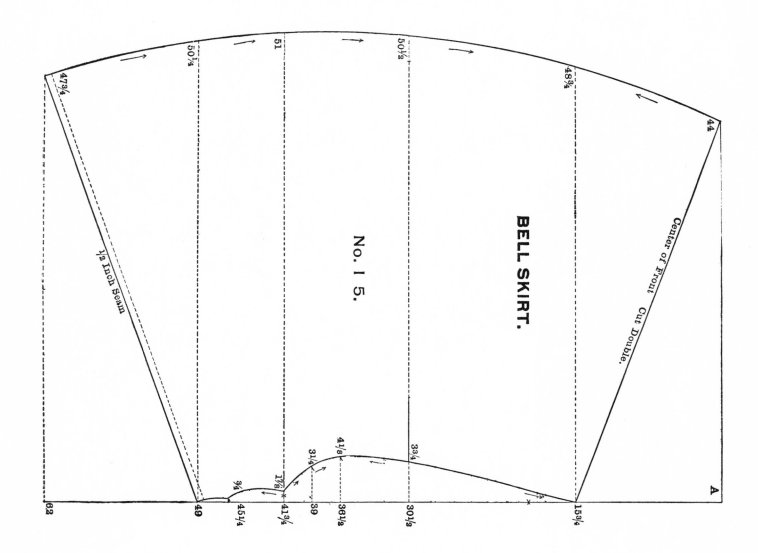

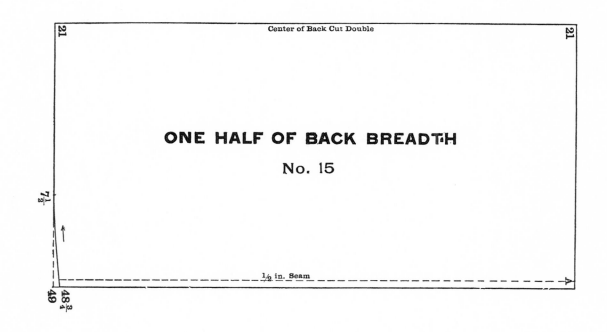

**ONE HALF OF BACK BREADTH**

No. 15

# LADIES' STREET COSTUME.
## Summer 1893

Use the scale corresponding with the Bust measure to draft the entire waist, which consists of Upper and Under-Front, Back, Side-Back, jacket Front and Back. Cut the Upper-Front double and fasten on the shoulder and under the arms. Gather the extra fullness at the waist and sew to a belt. The back of the jacket is cut double but rounded up from the bottom. The sleeves and skirt are given on page 44. Gather the top of the balloon sleeve and baste to the lining. Gather the extra fullness on the upper-side and baste in the seams. The Skirt is drafted by the waist measure. Gather the top, finish the bottom with a deep Spanish flounce. Make an extra flounce underneath with wiry goods to make it flare out. Regulate to suit.

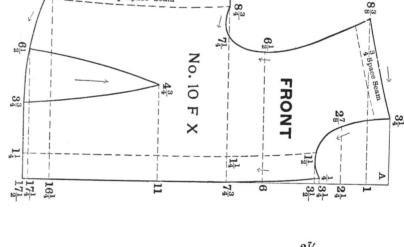

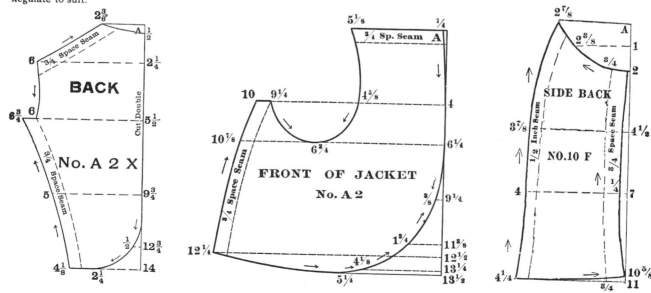

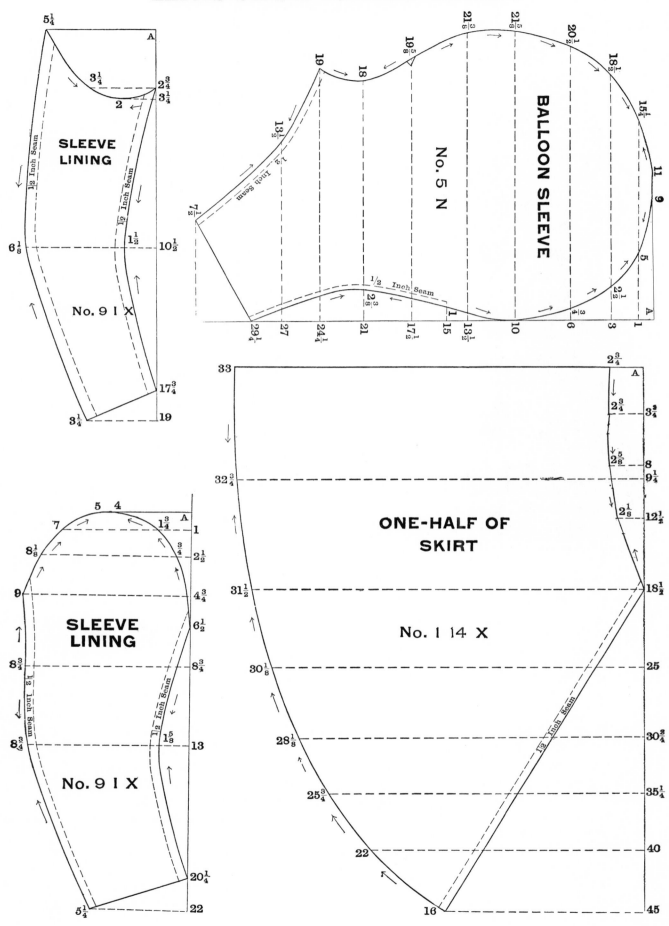

# LADIES' STREET COSTUME.
## Spring 1894

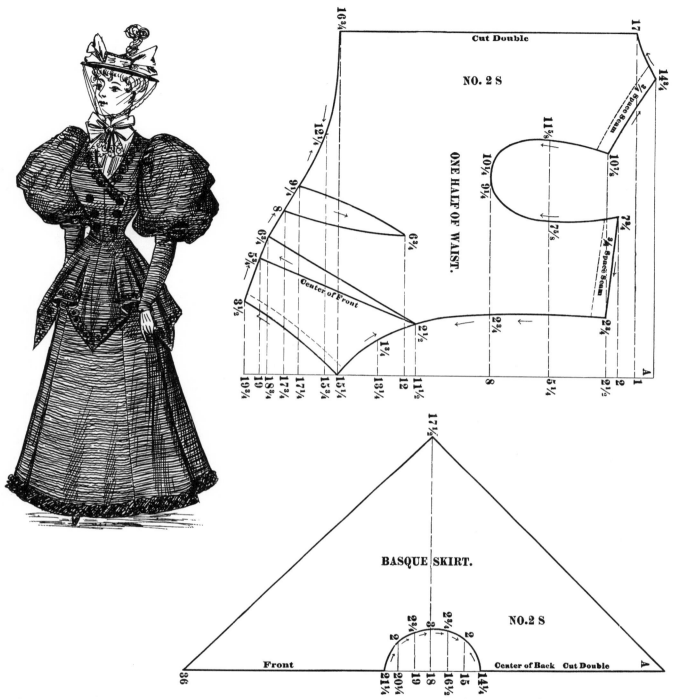

Use the scale corresponding with the Bust measure to draft the entire Basque, which consists of one-half of Waist and Basque Skirt. This is a novelty, but is very pretty when properly made. The Waist gives the seamless effect in the back, but has one dart on each side and one in the center of Front. The right Front may be cut off from 2½ down to 5¾. Close down the center of Front with hooks and eyes; lap the left Front over the right and button. Whalebone the lining under the arms and each dart.

Line the Basque Skirt with silk and sew to the waist, or finish with a band and hook the Waist to it; let it remain open down the front. It may be cut longer or shorter, just to suit.

The Sleeves are given on page 46, three pieces, upper and under Sleeve and Sleeve puff. Sew the puff on the dotted line.

The Skirt is given on page 47. Draft by the Waist measure. Is in three pieces, Front, Back and Side-gore. Put the parts together as they are marked. Any style of trimming may be used for the entire garment. Regulate the length by the tape measure.

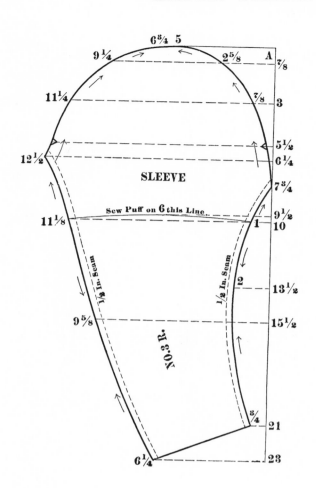

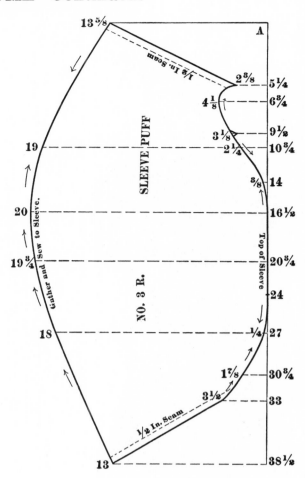

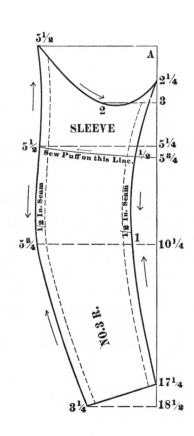

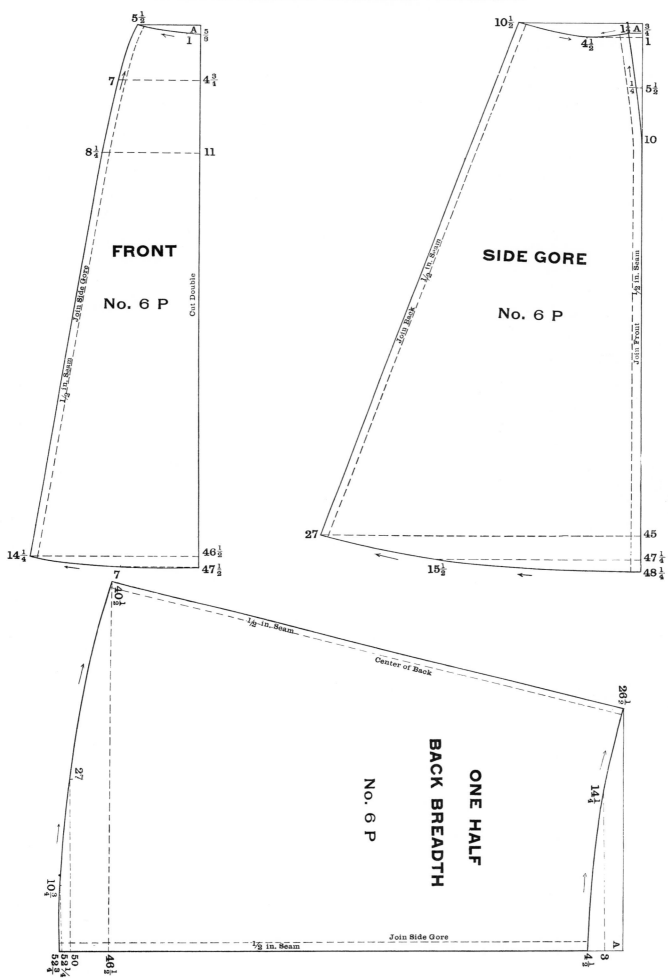

# LADIES' STREET COSTUME.
## Spring 1894

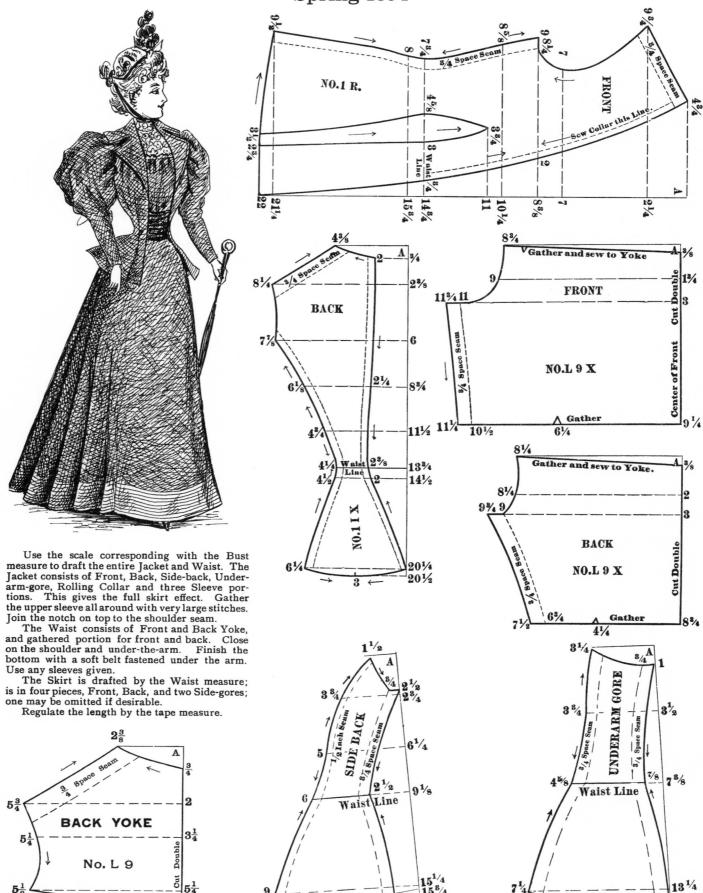

Use the scale corresponding with the Bust measure to draft the entire Jacket and Waist. The Jacket consists of Front, Back, Side-back, Under-arm-gore, Rolling Collar and three Sleeve portions. This gives the full skirt effect. Gather the upper sleeve all around with very large stitches. Join the notch on top to the shoulder seam.

The Waist consists of Front and Back Yoke, and gathered portion for front and back. Close on the shoulder and under-the-arm. Finish the bottom with a soft belt fastened under the arm. Use any sleeves given.

The Skirt is drafted by the Waist measure; is in four pieces, Front, Back, and two Side-gores; one may be omitted if desirable.

Regulate the length by the tape measure.

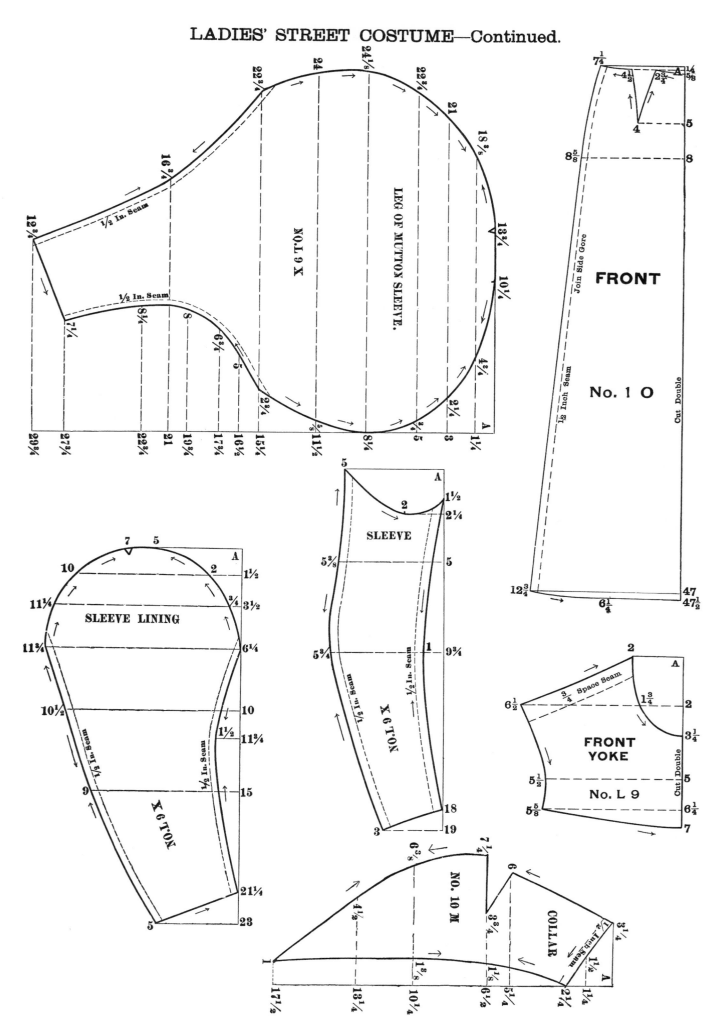

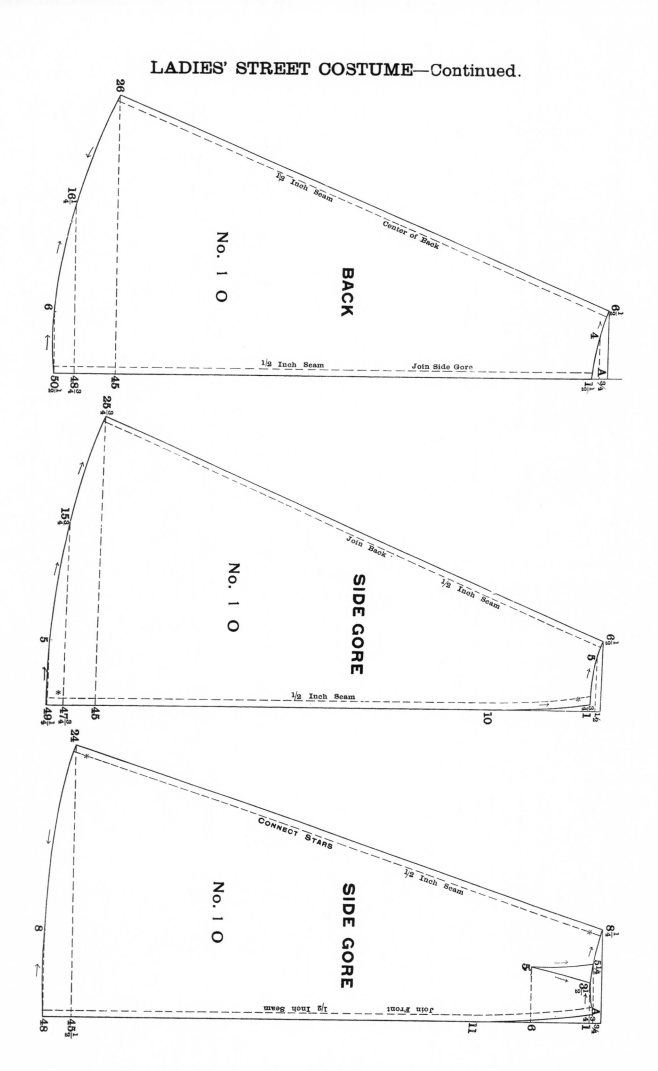

# MISSES' STREET COSTUME.
## Spring 1894

Use the scale corresponding with the Bust measure to draft the entire waist, which consists of Front and Back of Yoke, and gathered portions for Front and Back, Collar, Ruffle and two Sleeve portions. Gather the lower portion for the waist and sew to the yoke. The ruffle may be lined with silk and sewed in the same seam. Close down the front invisibly. Gather the sleeves to fit the arms eye.

The Skirt is given on page 53. Is in three pieces, Front, Back and Side-gore. Gather the top to fit the waist. Trim to suit.

Regulate the length by the tape measure.

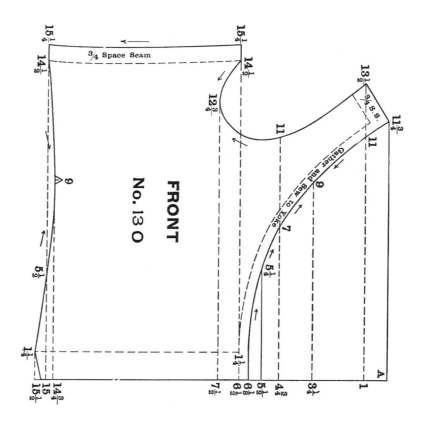

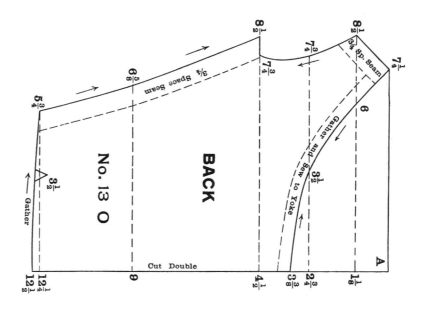

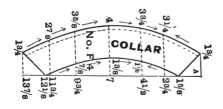

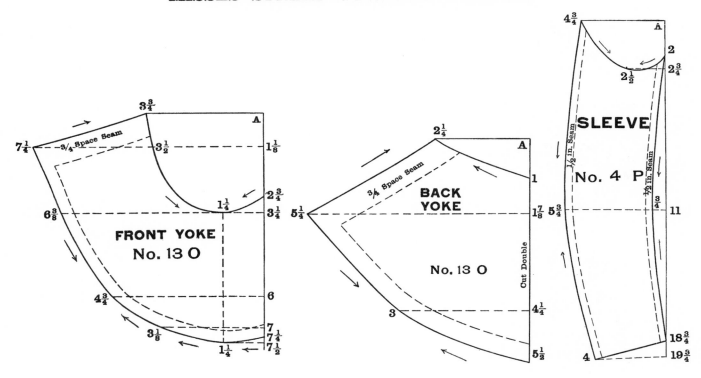

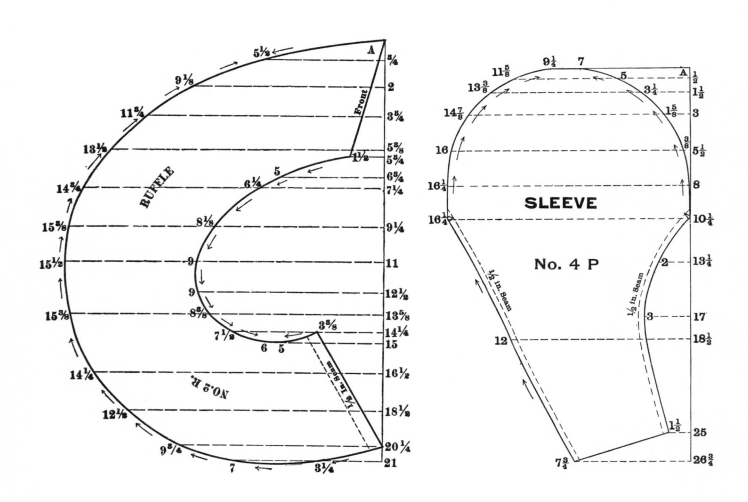

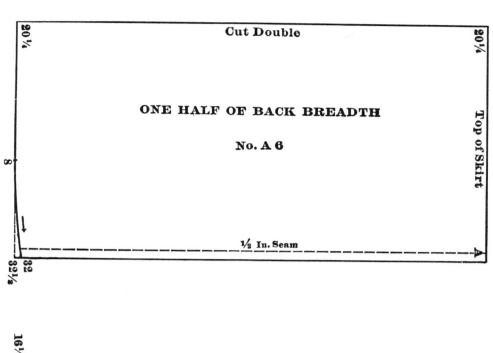

ONE HALF OF BACK BREADTH

No. A 6

Cut Double

Top of Skirt

½ In. Seam

20¼ · 20¼ · 8 · 32 · 32½

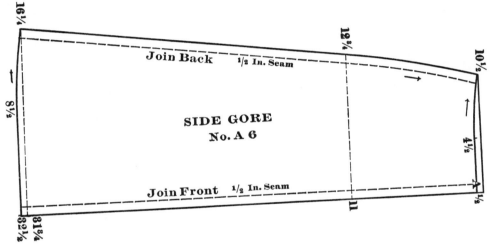

SIDE GORE
No. A 6

Join Back   ½ In. Seam

Join Front   ½ In. Seam

16¼ · 10½ · 8½ · 4½ · 12¾ · 11 · ½ · 31¾ · 32½

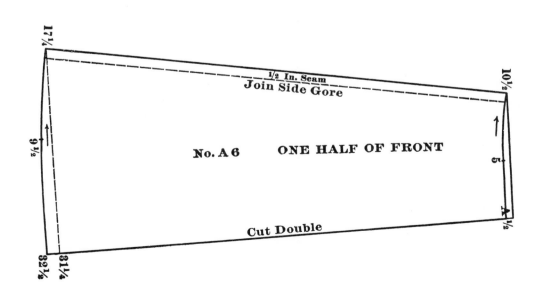

No. A 6   ONE HALF OF FRONT

½ In. Seam
Join Side Gore

Cut Double

17¼ · 10½ · 9½ · 5 · ½ · 31¼ · 32½

# LADIES' STREET COSTUME.
## Spring 1894

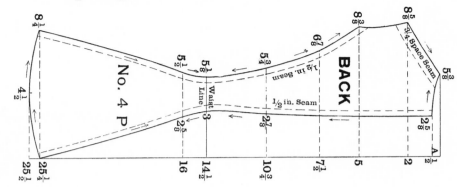

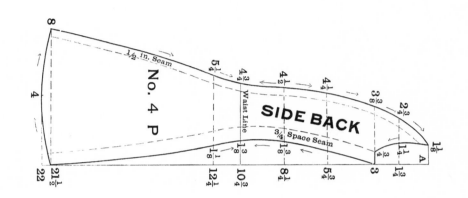

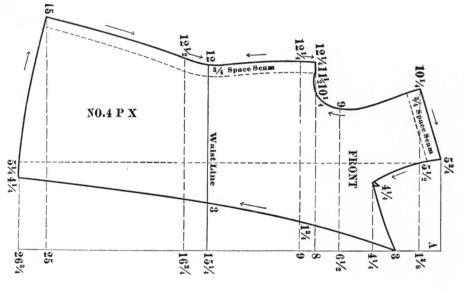

Use the scale corresponding with the Bust measure to draft the entire Jacket and Waist. The Jacket consists of Front, Back, Side-back, Under-arm-gore, Rolling Collar and two Sleeve portions. This gives the full skirt. Make as long as desirable. May be made of any suitable material; face the Front and turn back. The full Waist in given on page 55, it consists of Front and Back. Gather the top to fit the neck. It may be made up over a lining. Gather the bottom and finish with a soft belt.

The Skirt is given on page 56. Draft by the Waist measure. Is in two pieces, Front and Back. Gather the center of Back from the notch.

A very pretty finish for the bottom of Skirts is made by cutting bias velvet 1½ inches wide and making a heavy cord by twisting candle wick loosely, covering it with the velvet. Sew it on the bottom and face the under side of the Skirt.

Regulate the length of the Skirt by the tape msasure.

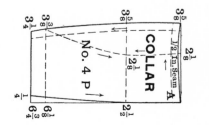

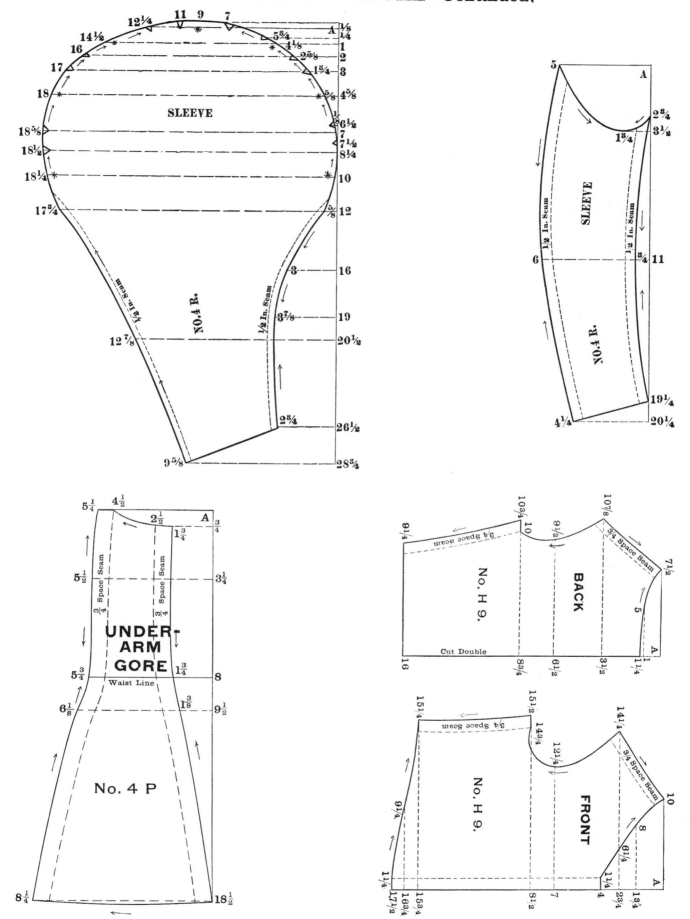

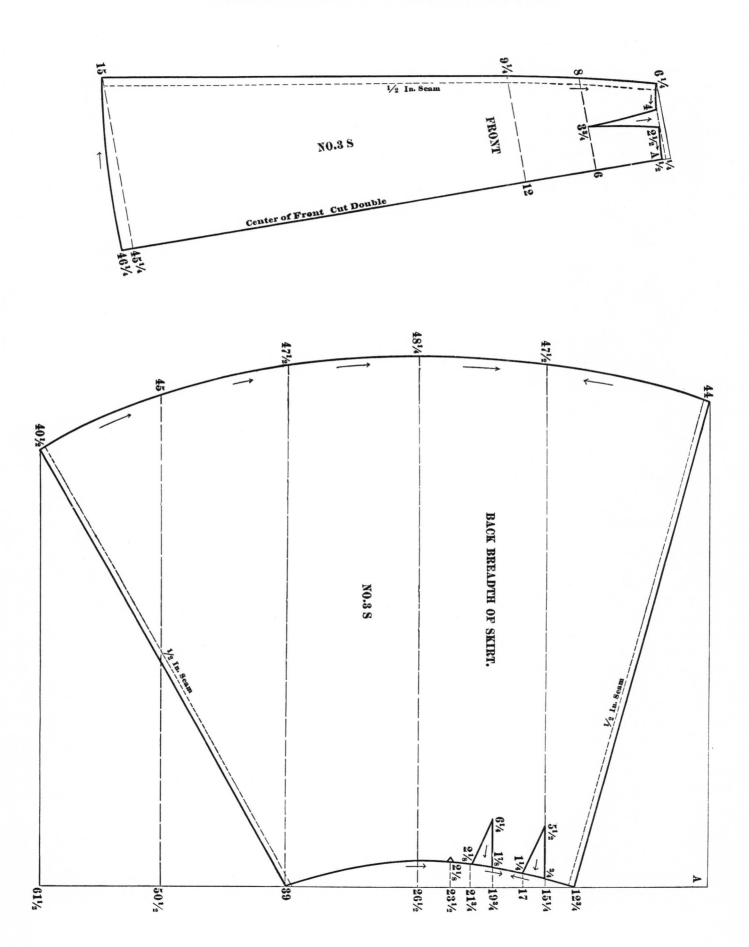

# LADIES' STREET GOWN
## Spring 1894

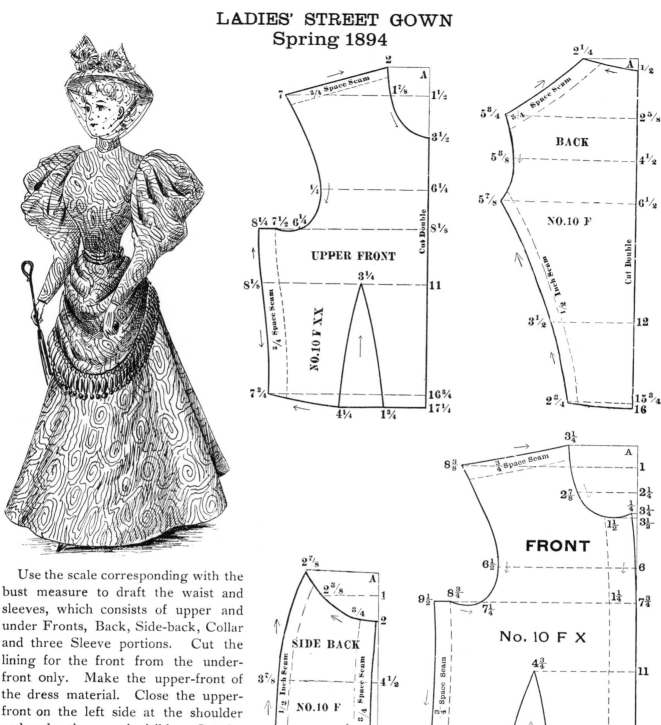

Use the scale corresponding with the bust measure to draft the waist and sleeves, which consists of upper and under Fronts, Back, Side-back, Collar and three Sleeve portions. Cut the lining for the front from the under-front only. Make the upper-front of the dress material. Close the upper-front on the left side at the shoulder and under the arm invisibly. Cut the back double, gather very coarsely or pleat the upper sleeve between the notches. The drapery and skirt are drafted by the Waist measure. The drapery is in two pieces, Front and Back. Lay three upward turning pleats in the front drapery. Lay three backward turning pleats in the back. Face the front edge with silk or velvet and turn back on the outside to form a revere. The same trimming may trim the front drapery—The effect is very pleasing. The skirt is a Bell skirt, any other full skirt may be used if desirable. Regulate the length by the tape measure.

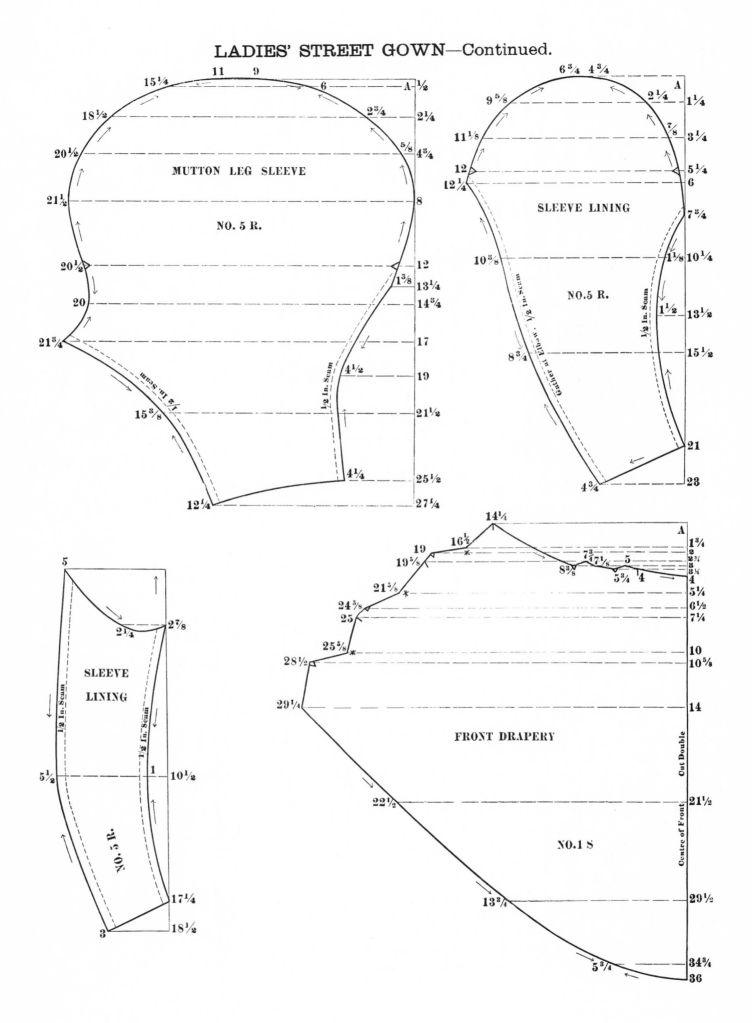

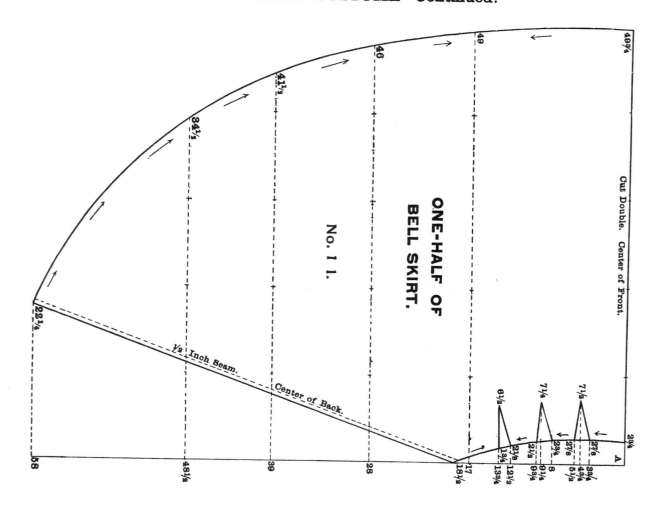

ONE-HALF OF
BELL SKIRT.

No. 11.

Cut Double. Center of Front.

½ Inch Seam.

Center of Back.

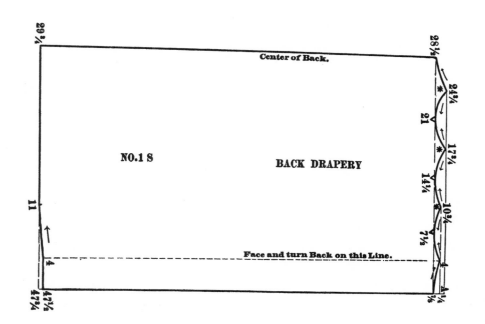

NO. 18      BACK DRAPERY

Center of Back.

Face and turn Back on this Line.

# LADIES' STREET COSTUME.
## Spring 1895

Use the scale corresponding with the bust measure to draft the waist and sleeves, which consists of Front, Back, Side-back, Under-arm-gore, two revere portions, vest front and three sleeve portions.

This is a short pointed basque; draft the same as all other garments. The revere or large collar may be made separately; interline with canvas, finish the edge with guimp or jet trimming. The bottom of the basque may be finished with a soft roll of velvet or silk finish, the back with a butterfly bow.

The sleeves may be pleated in various ways, or gathered; one of the prettiest ways is to lay side pleats, meeting in the center or at point of shoulder.

Another is to make a box pleat on top with deep side pleats on each side. Always line the puff part with crinoline, tarletan or fibre chamois, the latter is the most durable as the coat sleeve will not crush it.

The skirt is drafted by the waist measure, it consists of front, back breadth and side-gore. Line the back with hair-cloth and make a double box pleat down the center. The effect is very pretty and more durable than the Godet pleats, or it may be gathered or pleated in deep knife pleats, meeting at the center.

Regulate the length by the tape measure.

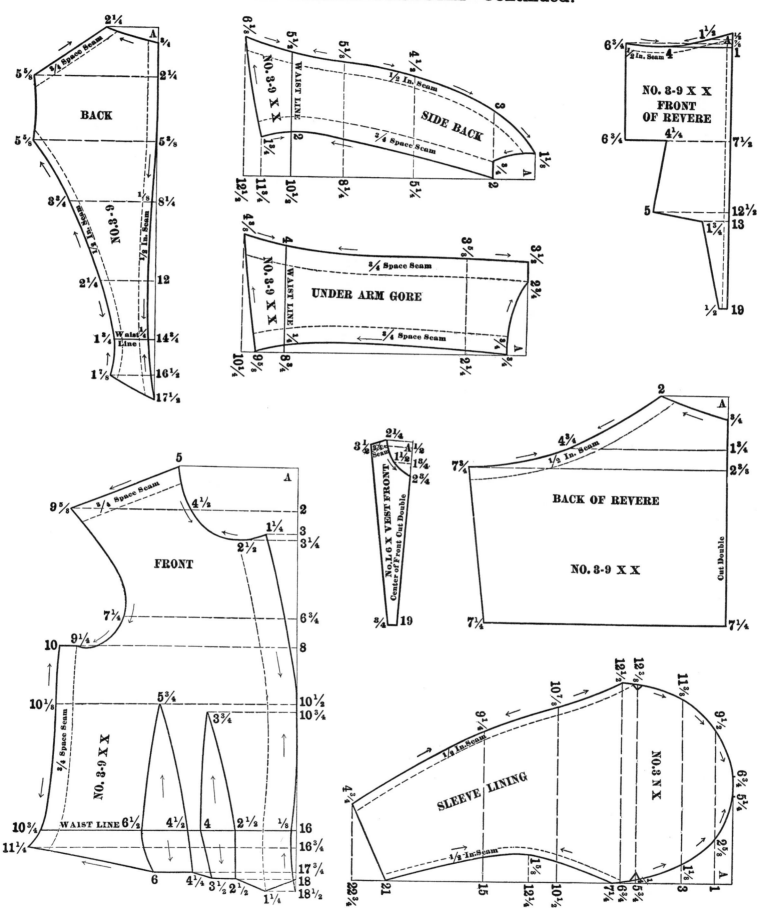

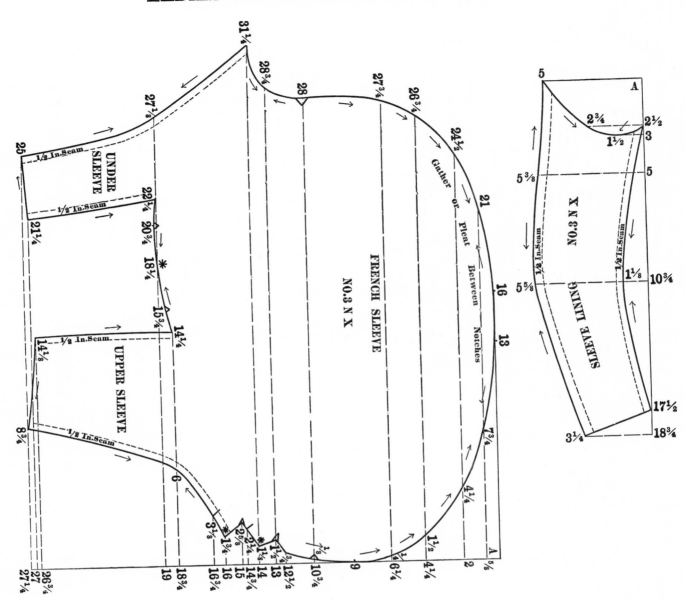

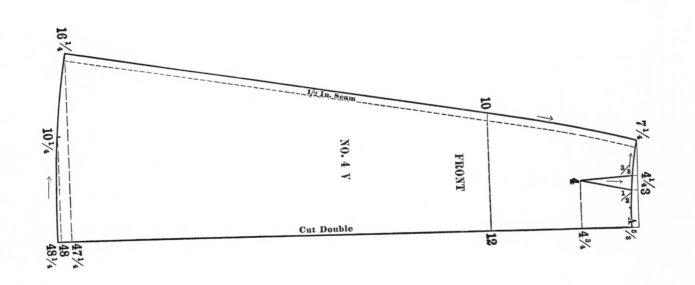

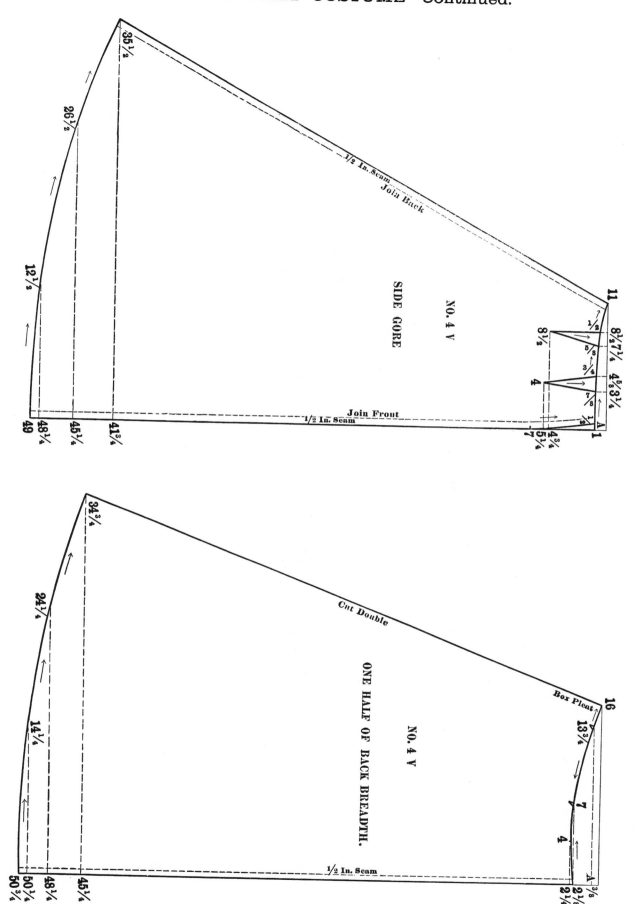

# LADIES' STREET COSTUME.
## Spring 1895

Use the scale corresponding with the bust measure to draft the entire waist, which consists of two fronts, back, vest front, waist trimming, and three sleeve portions. Draft same as all others. Cut the French back double, take up the darts in the large front (which may be made of the lining only) close down the center with hooks and eyes. The back and small front may be made of velvet, also the trimmings. Lay pleats to form a cascade. The vest front is given on page 66. Make of perforated cloth or velvet. Lay the sleeve puff in three double box pleats; interline with Tarletan or Fibre Chamois. Gather the bottom and sew to the sleeve lining on the dotted lines. Draft the drapery and skirt by the waist measure.

The drapery or cascade is given on page 66. Face all around with the same material as the skirt. Lay the pleats to form a cascade; join to the front seams. The skirt is given on page 67. Is in three pieces — front, back breadths, and side-gore. Gather or pleat the back. Face the bottom with hair cloth 13 inches deep. Bind the bottom with velvet. Regulate the length with the tape measure.

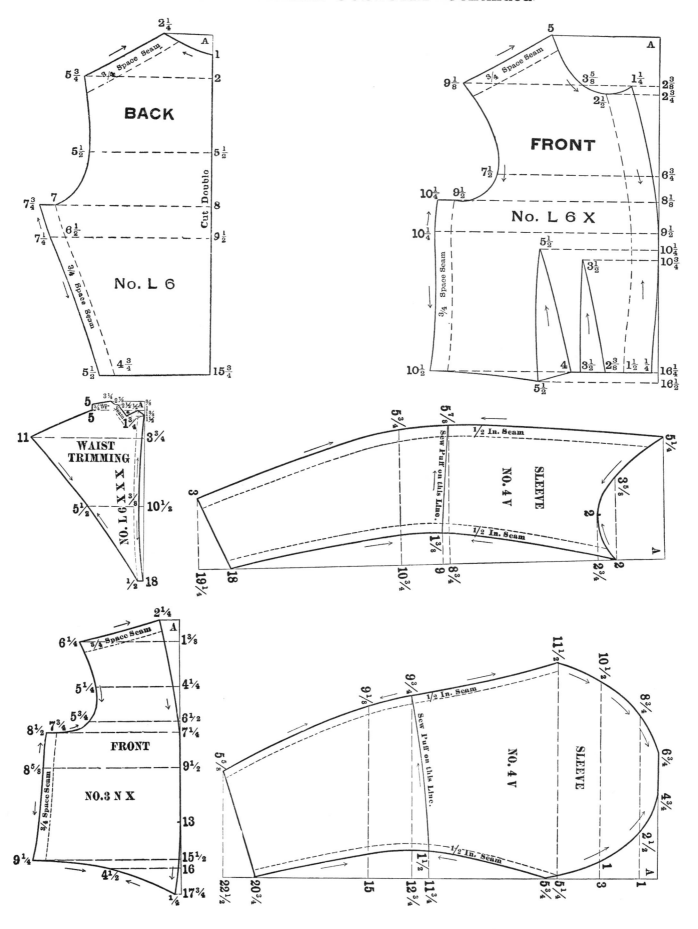

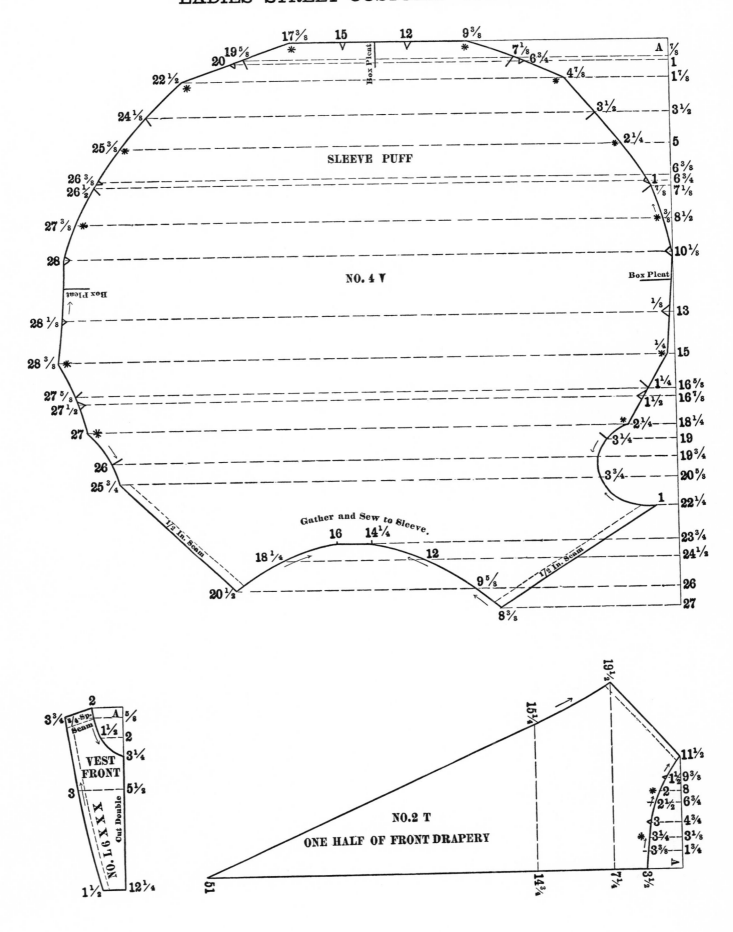

SLEEVE PUFF

NO. 4 ▼

Box Pleat

Gather and Sew to Sleeve.

1½ In. Seam

1½ In. Seam

VEST
FRONT

NO. 9 XXX

Out Double

NO. 2 T
ONE HALF OF FRONT DRAPERY

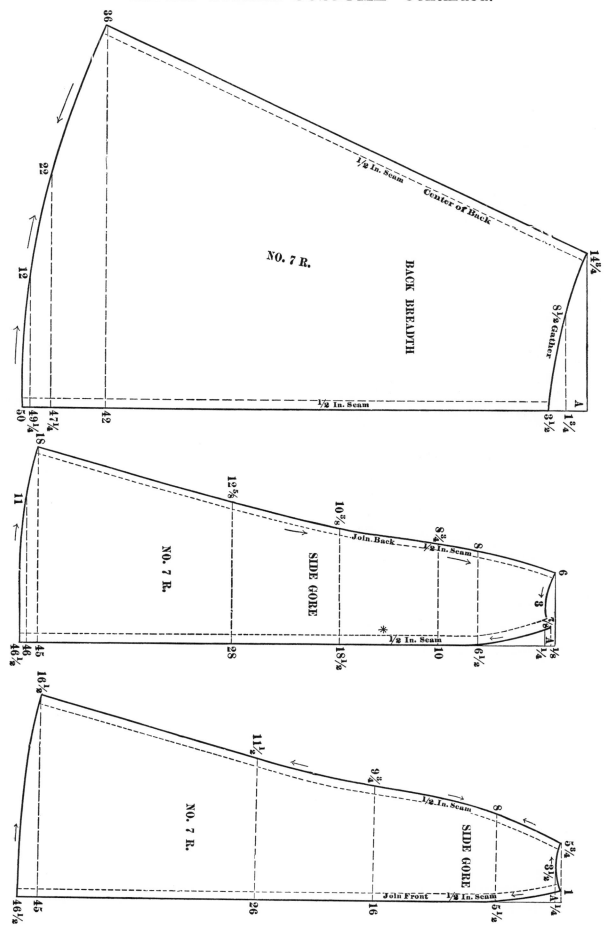

# LADIES' STREET COSTUME.
## Spring 1895

Use the scale corresponding with the bust measure to draft the entire waist and sleeves, which consists of 2 fronts, back, collar, and three sleeve portions.

Cut the under front lining from the diagram having only one dart. Close with hooks and eyes. Cut a lining to the upper front also, and close on the left shoulder and under the arm with hooks and eyes. If the lady for whom this waist is being cut is slender, the darts in the upper front may be omitted. Cut the material on the bias, and baste it to the under front down the center (very firmly) and stretch it to fit the figure. It can be easily done if the figure is good. Cut off the surplus goods at the bottom and under the arms after it has been firmly basted all around. Trim with braiding, same as represented, or any other style. Interline the sleeve puff with Tarletan or Fibre Chamois, and sew to the sleeve lining.

The skirt is given on page 70. Draft by the waist measure. It consists of front, and Godet pleat for the back. There may be two, three or four of these, as they are all cut alike; we have given but one. Interline the back throughout with haircloth. The front may be faced up to the knee with the same. Stay the pleats underneath with elastic. Do not press them, however.

Trim the front with light and dark cloth. Cut in strips pointed at the ends, and finish with nail heads, or any other decoration. Regulate the length by the tape measure.

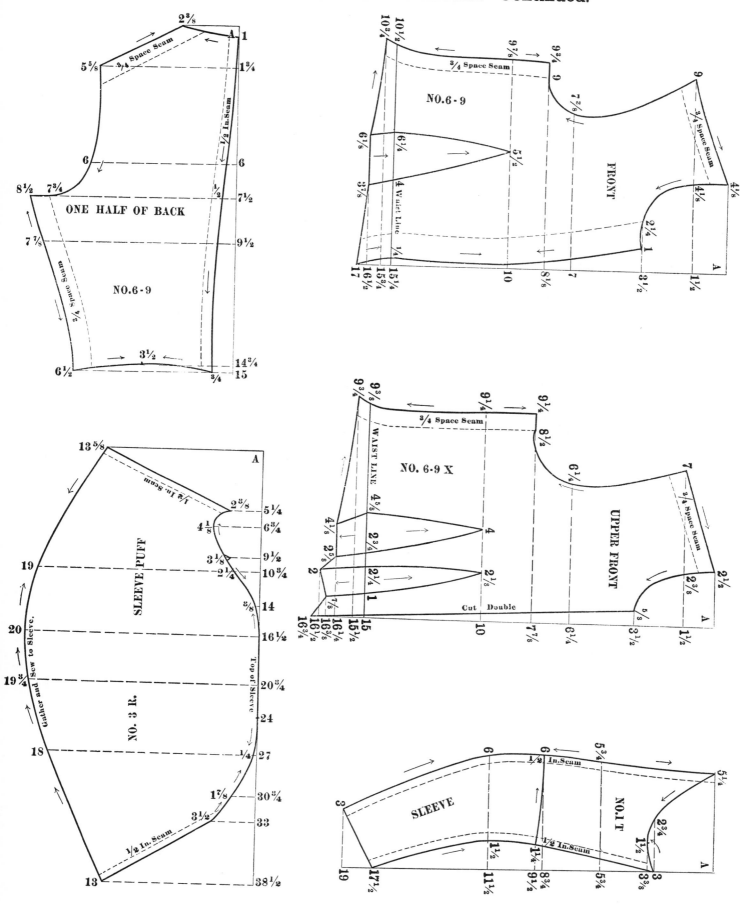

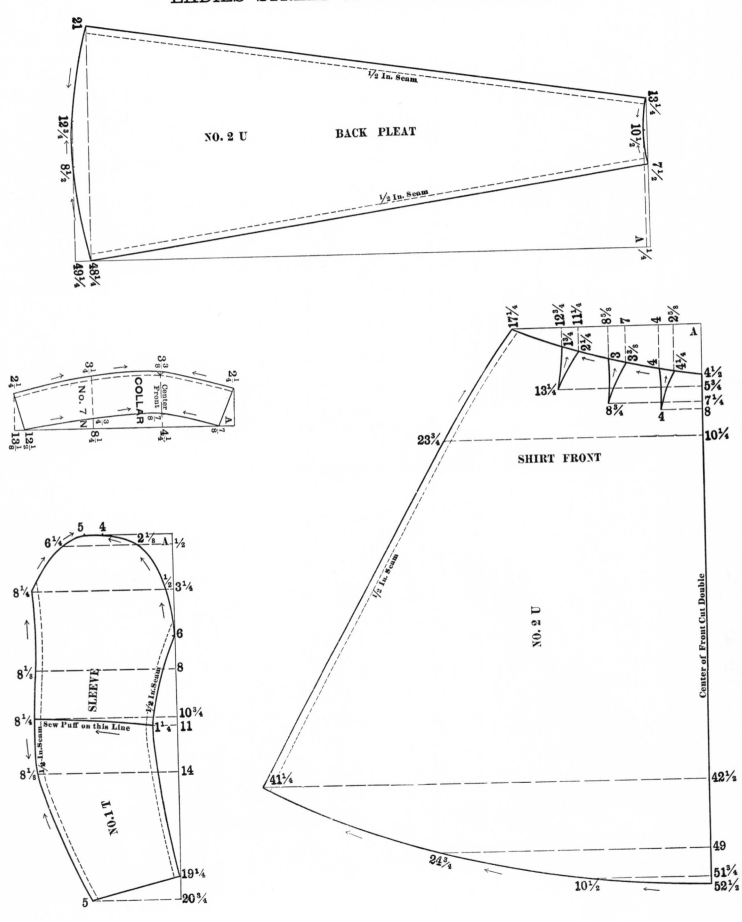

# LADIES' STREET COSTUME.
## Winter 1896

### *LADIES' STREET COSTUME.*

Use the scale corresponding with the bust measure to draft the entire Jacket, which consists of Front, Back, Side-back, Under-arm Gore, and five Sleeve portions.

This Jacket is tight fitting in the Back and loose in Front. It also gives the ripple skirt, corresponding with the present style. If it is made of light weight cloth, interline throughout with heavy fibre chamois, which will give warmth and a finish that no other material will. The outer lining should be of taffeta silk, harmonizing in color. The Melon Sleeve is given on Page 73; this is drafted the same as any other garment; it also should be interlined with fibre chamois. Put the parts together according to the stars and numbers. Each seam should be corded with a contrasting color. Lay Box Pleats at the top, according to the notches and little straight lines. This Sleeve may also be used for a Dress Sleeve. The Skirt is given on Pages 74 and 75; draft by the scale corresponding with the Waist. Measure is in four pieces, Front, Back and two Side Gores; this gives the ripple effect. If it is not the desired width, add one more side gore; if this is done, make the top of each a trifle smaller. Face the bottom the depth of ten inches, with hair cloth. Use cotton taffeta to line the Skirt. Regulate the length by the tape measure.

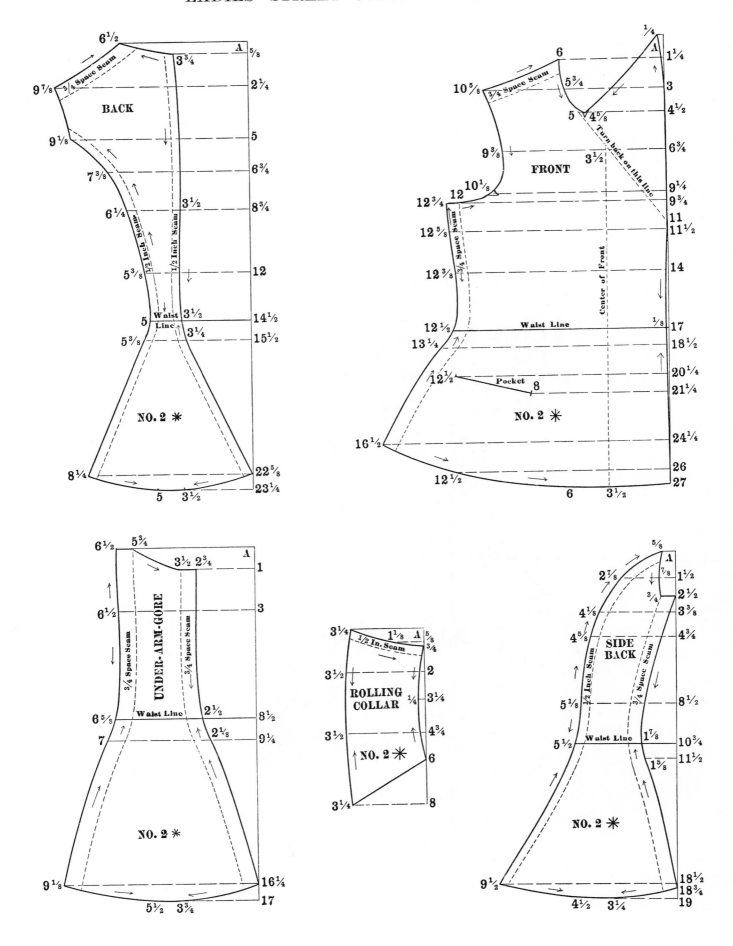

# LADIES' MELON SLEEVE.

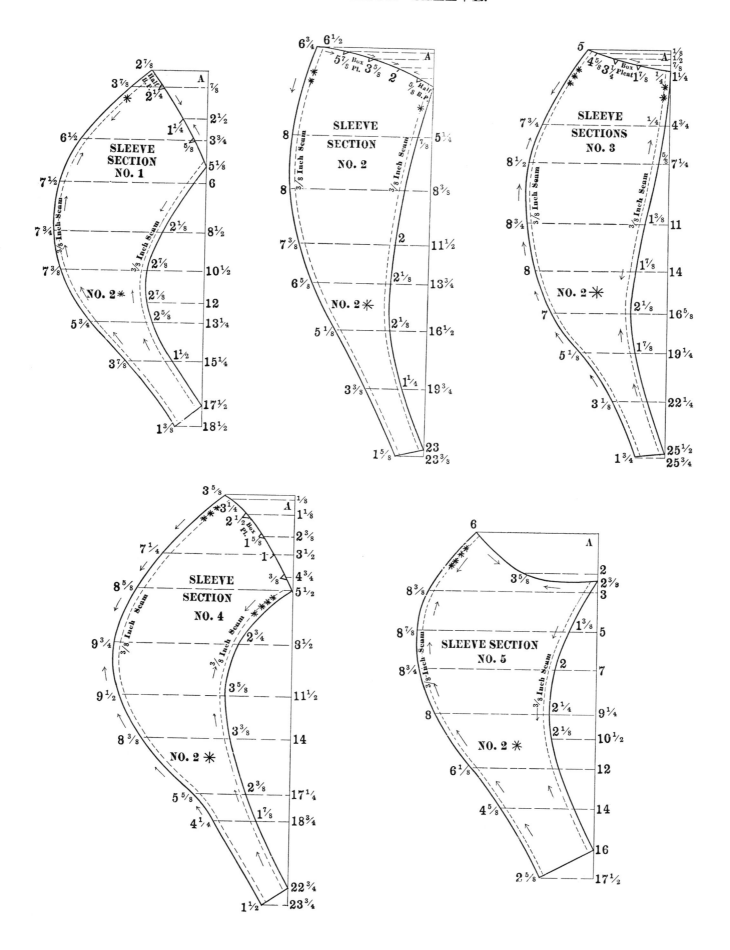

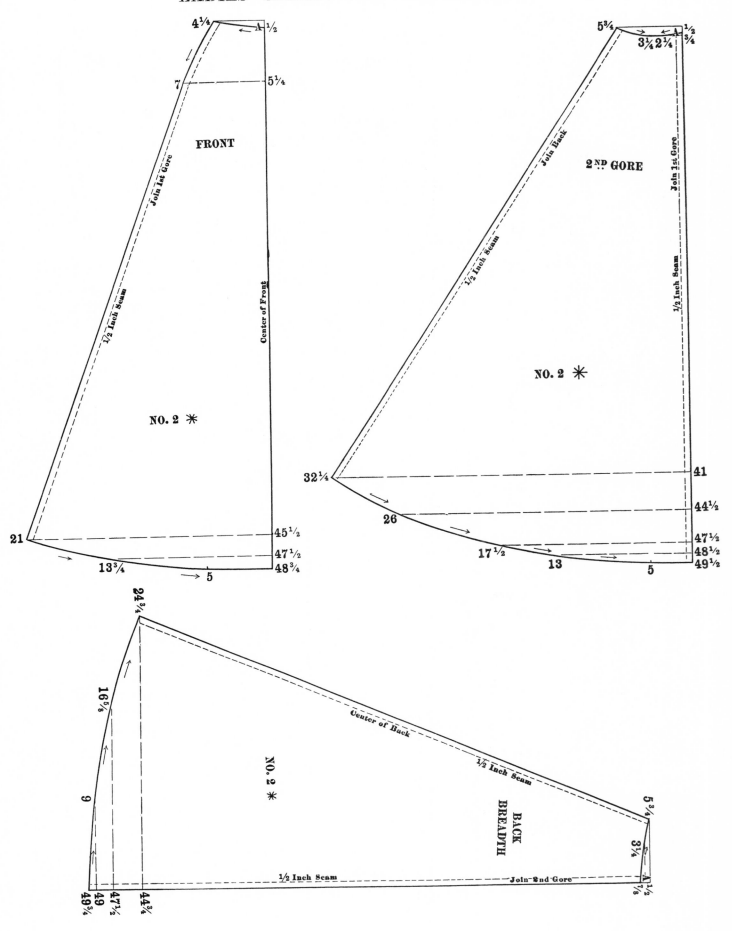

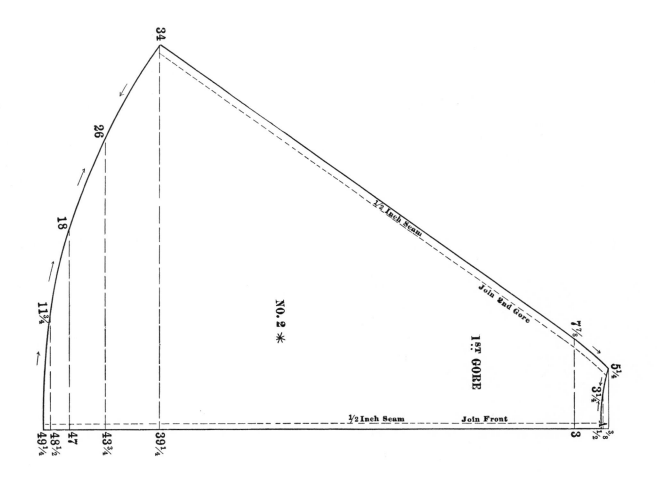

# LADIES' STREET COSTUME.
## Winter 1896

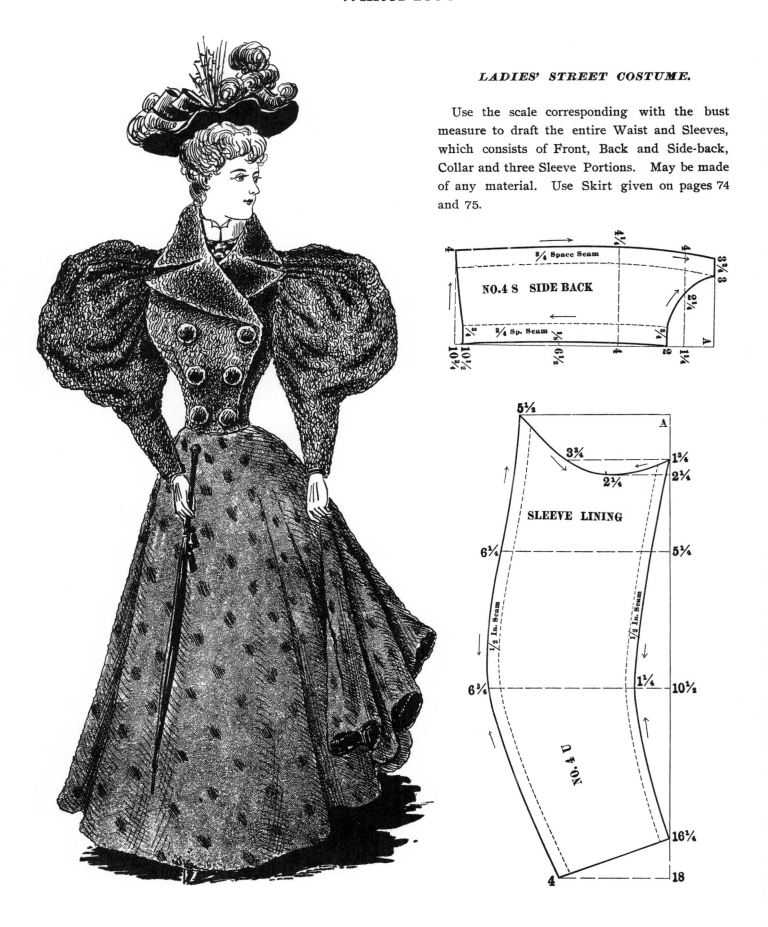

***LADIES' STREET COSTUME.***

Use the scale corresponding with the bust measure to draft the entire Waist and Sleeves, which consists of Front, Back and Side-back, Collar and three Sleeve Portions. May be made of any material. Use Skirt given on pages 74 and 75.

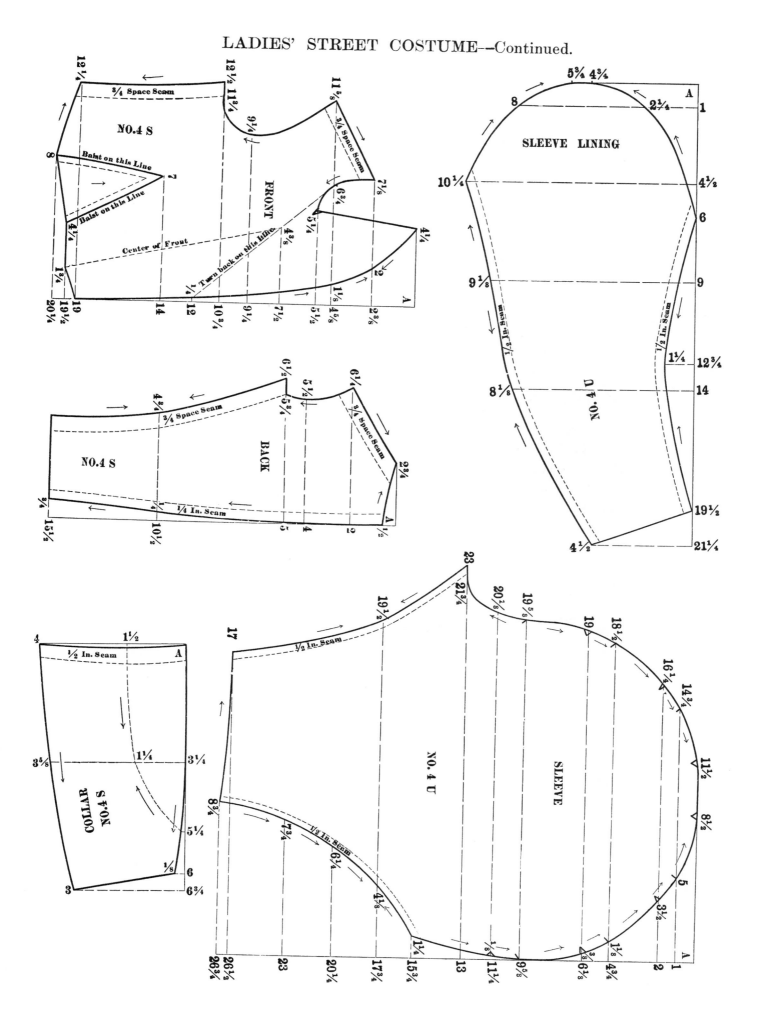

# LADIES' COSTUME.
## Fall 1890

The object in inserting this draft in the quarterly magazine is to accommodate those of our patrons who do not fully understand our method of drafting. In the first place, we ascertain the correct measures.

It is impossible to obtain a perfect-fitting garment with incorrect measurement. Therefore we insist that to obtain the desired results we must be accurate in taking the measures.

First, take the bust measure with the tape-line straight around the largest part of the bust, high up under the arms; take snug, close measure, neither too tight nor too loose.

Take measure around the waist as tight as the dress is to be worn. Take length of waist from the large joint where the neck and body join down to the waist. Care must be taken to get this measure. If it is difficult, as it often is, to ascertain just where to locate the waist line in the back, take a belt or string and place around the waist, very tight, as low down as the dress can be worn.

Sleeve measure is taken from the center of back to wrist joint, with arm raised and elbow bent.

Always draft the back first, as our measures are taken from the back.

After obtaining the bust measure, select from the package of scales the corresponding scale, and place it on the square; fasten securely with the screw, then square the paper by drawing a pencil-mark across the top and down the side of the square. Then proceed to draw out the pattern. First make points on the paper corresponding with all the figures on the outside of the base-line until you come to 14¼, which is the waist line. Now make a dot with the pencil at 14¼. Take the tape-line and measure from the point you have made at ¾ down to 14¼, or waist line, and if it does not correspond with the tape-line measurement, raise or lower the point and draw the waist line from there. Take the scale and measure the difference between the dot made at 14¼ and the point for the waist-line, and change the waist-line on the side, back and front the same amount. If you have raised or lowered the waist-line one or two spaces, as the case may be, change all the figures below the waist-line correspondingly.

Be very accurate in getting the cross-figures, as sometimes an eighth of a space added to or taken from makes it impossible to obtain a true curve. If the eighths were not essential they would not have been placed there. Remember this. Put them down just as they occur on the different diagrams. It is useless to explain how to lay the curve to draft out the basque, for the different changes are given in full on the diagrams for the back, side-back, front and two-sleeves, and all others are gotten in the same way. The arrow-head points toward the largest part of the curve; therefore, if you notice which way the arrow points, you will at once know how to lay the curve.

We next draft the side-back. Square the paper as previously explained. Make a point at all the figures as they occur on the base-line until you come to 10¼, or waist-line. Change this the same as on the back. Do not use the tape line to measure the side-back or front, but change the waist-lines just the same amount, either up or down, as the case may be. If you have raised or lowered the waist-line one or two spaces, raise or lower all the figures on the base-line below the waist-line the same amount as waist-line. Put the figures down on the cross-line just as they occur on the diagram. Then take the curve and draw out the pattern.

Draft the front next. Square the paper and proceed as before, making a point for all the figures on the base-line until you come to 16, or waist-line. If you have raised or lowered the waist-line on the back and side-back, also change this to correspond, and change all the figures below the waist-line the same. Put the figures down just as they occur on the cross-lines; then take the curve and draw out the pattern.

Measure the waist of the entire basque with the tape-line, omitting all seams, darts and hem if it does not correspond with the desired waist measure. Add to or take from the under-arm dart one-half the amount required. Do not cut the dart out; baste on the lines here given. Where the darts are very bias, cut them open through the center. All seams should be slashed in at the waist-line to prevent drawing. Be careful to connect the waist-lines. In basting the side-back and back together, hold the side-back towards you. Put all the extra fullness over the shoulder blades. In basting the shoulder seams, stretch the front two or three inches from the neck.

Better results can be obtained in fitting the waist

# LADIES' COSTUME—Continued.

by not basting the hem down the front before trying it on. Never put it on wrong side out. Baste all the seams up and slash them at the waist-lines. Then put it on the person to be fitted. Pin the fronts together just as you would were it to be sewed together, commencing at the waist-line, drawing it as tight as the garment is to be worn,

paying no attention to the swell front on the pattern.

This way you will obtain an accurate shape of the waist, bust and neck. Before taking the pins out mark with pencil or chalk. Turn down half an inch from this line on the right side for the button-holes.

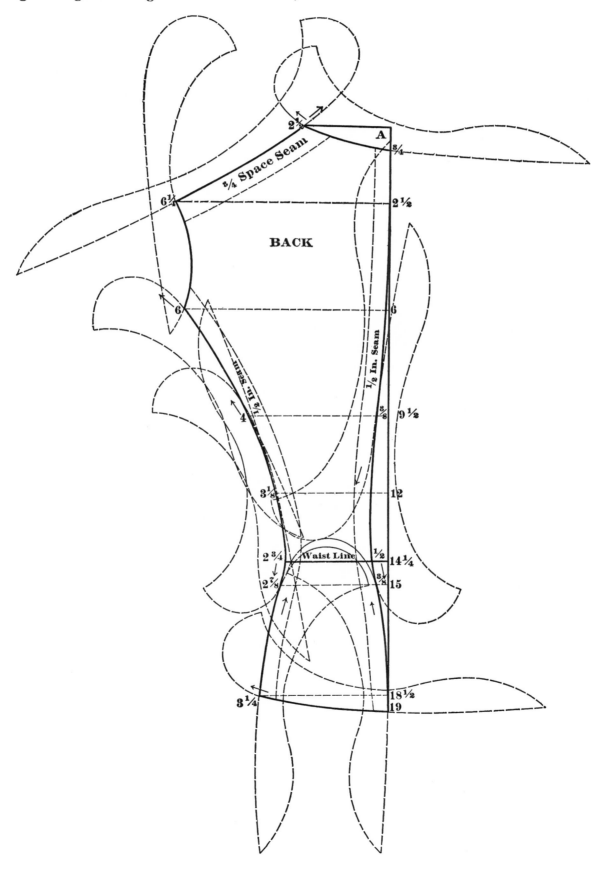

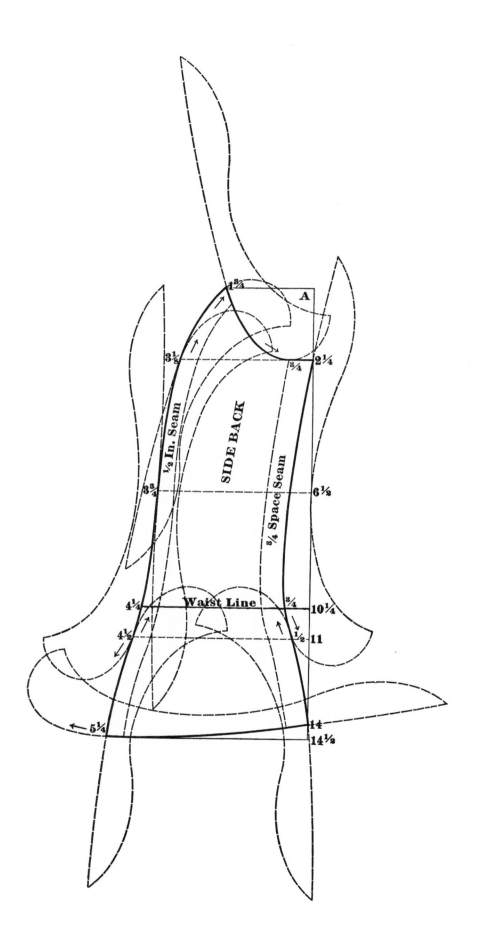

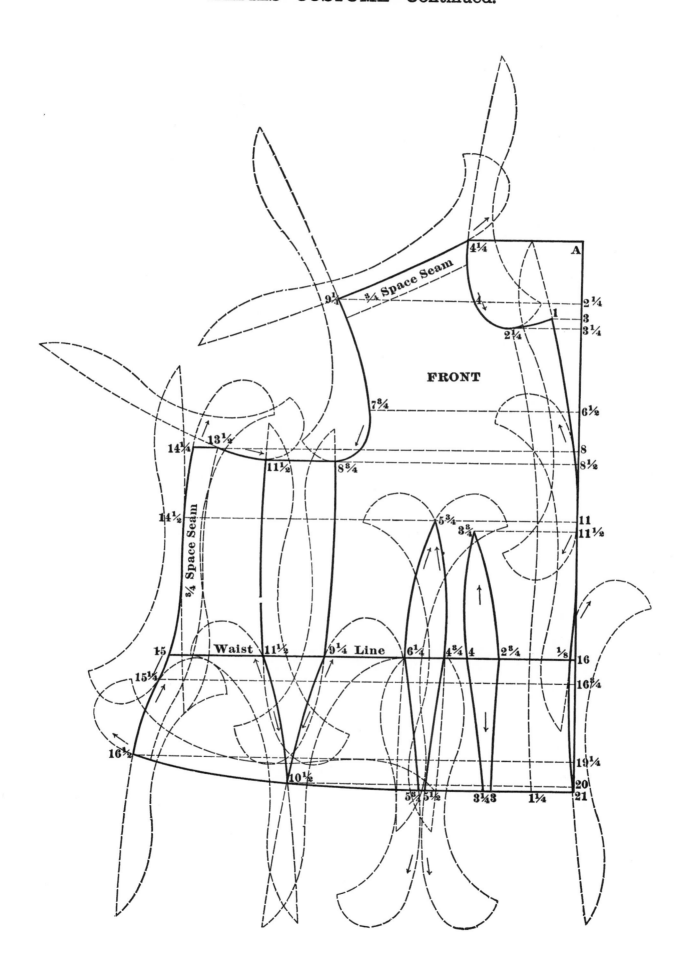

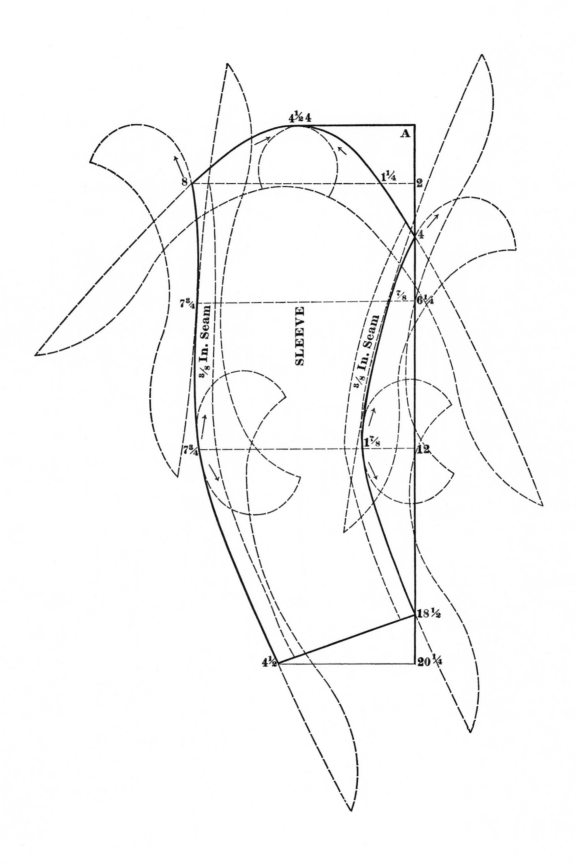

Take measure for the sleeve with the arm raised and elbow bent; measure from center of back to knuckle joint. Deduct width of back piece, less one inch for seams. This gives correct length of sleeve.

Then square the paper as we have previously explained, make a mark for all the figures outside of the base line, then proceed to get the figures on the cross lines.

Take the tape line and measure the upper sleeve from 8 on back of sleeve down to 4½ at the bottom. If it is not the required length, change the two lower figures on the base line, 18½ and 20¼, either up or down, to correspond with tape line measurement. If we have changed it two or three spaces, change the line at the elbow one-half the distance.

Draft the under part of the sleeve the same way. If the figures have been changed on the upper sleeve, change the lower figures on the under part to correspond.

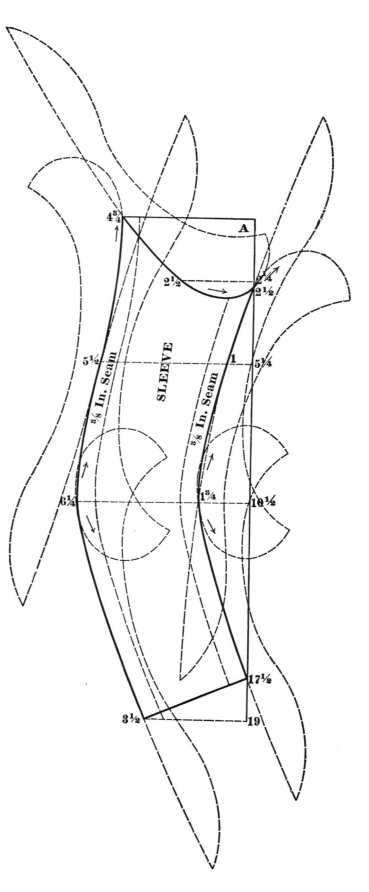

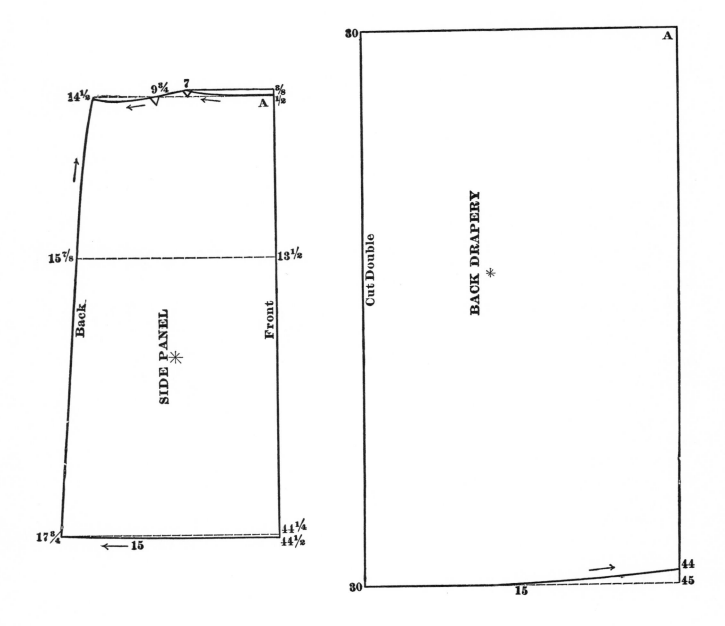

The Drapery and Skirt is drafted by the scale corresponding with the waist measure. The drapery is in two pieces—Side-Panel and Back. Gather the back drapery, interline the panel, and lay one pleat over the hip. Make just the same length as the skirt.

The Skirt consists of three pieces—Front, Back and Side-Gore. Draft this upon the general plan of work. Regulate the length with the tape measure.

This completes the instruction draft, and all the others are drafted upon the same plan. Be accurate in putting down the figures and follow the arrows closely.

# LADIES' PLAIN SKIRT.

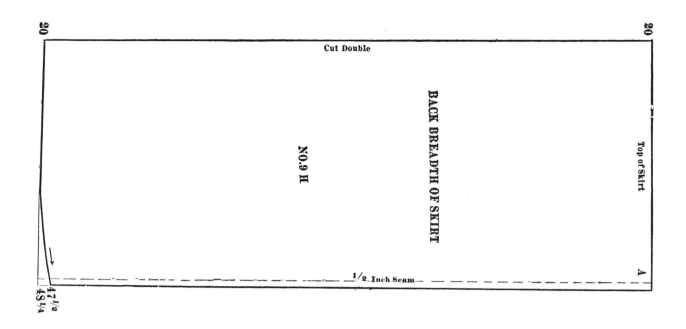

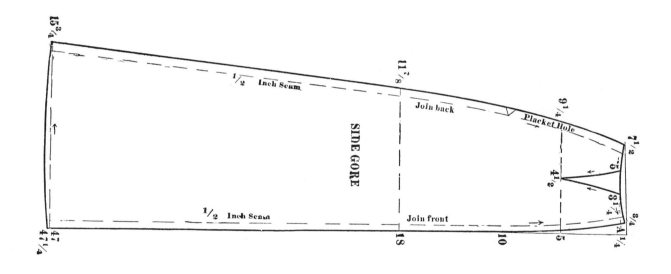

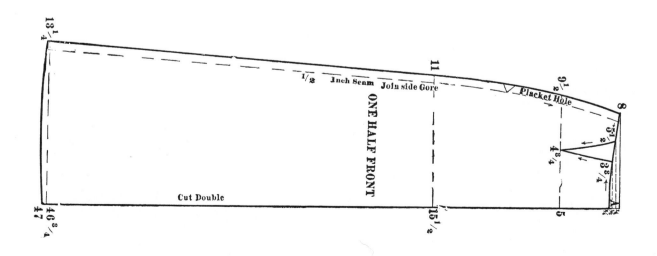

# LADIES' COSTUME.
## Fall 1890

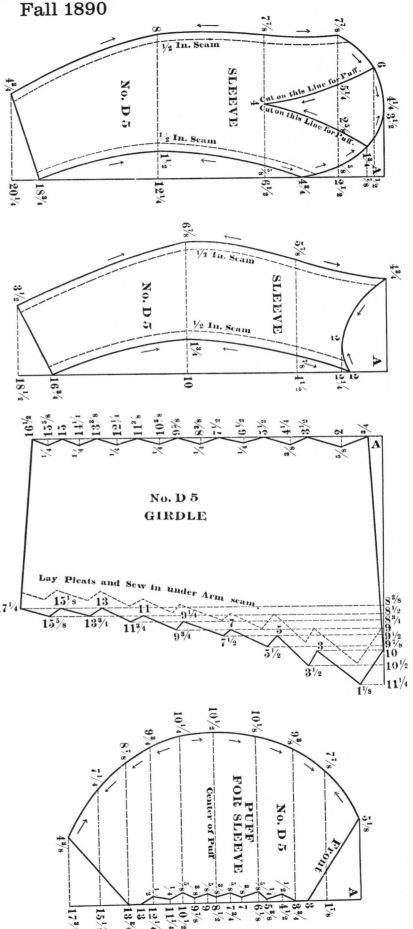

### LADIES' COSTUME.

Use the scale corresponding with the bust measure to draft the waist and sleeves, which consists of ten pieces— Upper and Under Fronts, Upper and Under Backs, Side-Back, Under-Arm Gore, Pleated Girdle, Puff for the Sleeves, and two Sleeve Portions.

Lay pleats at the bottom of the upper back and front according to the notches.

Lay the pleats and sew the girdle in the under-arm seam. Close in front with a large buckle.

Draft the sleeves same as any other sleeves, but to make as represented: cut out the upper sleeves as diagrams show, turn under each side and insert the pleated puff; lay the pleats toward the center line, gather at the top and sew in the arms eye; trim the sleeve at the hand same as the skirt or with a cuff.

The skirt is given on page 88, is drafted by the scale corresponding with waist measure, is in one piece; bring most of the fullness in the back.

Regulate the length by the tape measure.

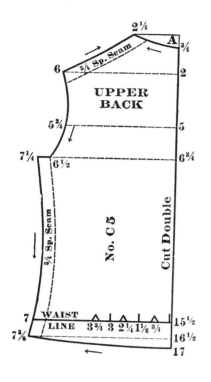

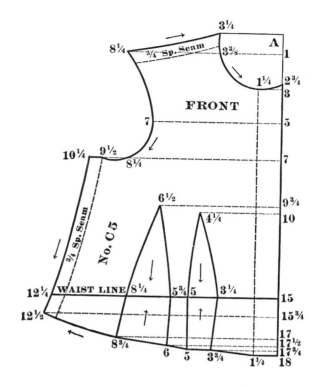

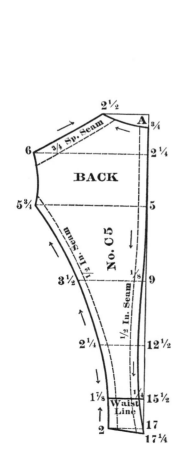

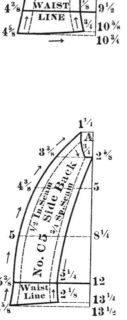

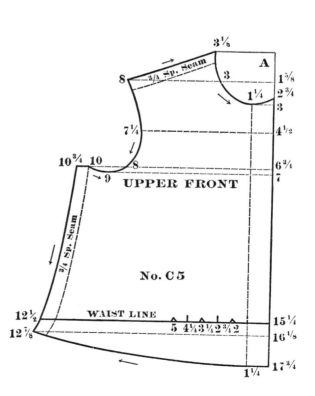

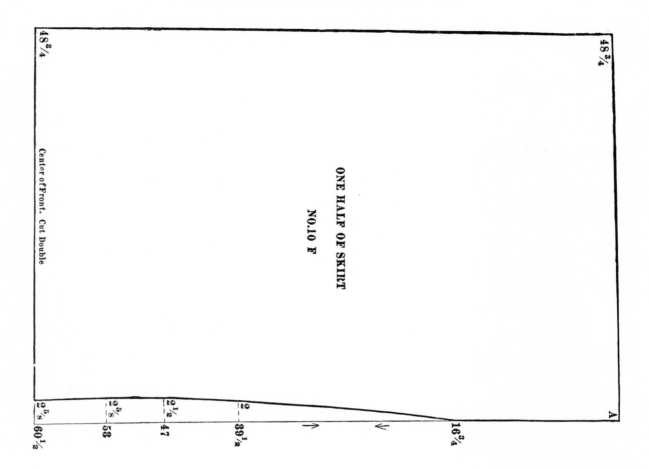

ONE HALF OF SKIRT

NO.10 F

Center of Front. Cut Double

48 3/4

48 3/4

A

16 3/4

2 — 39 1/2

2 1/2 — 47

2 5/8 — 58

2 5/8 — 60 1/2

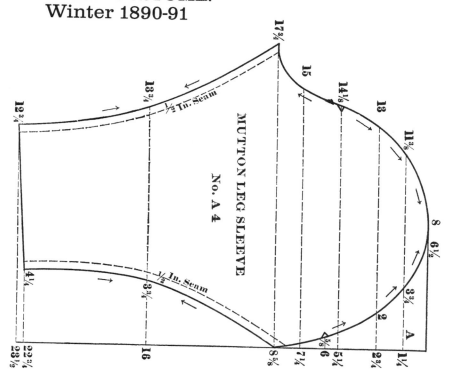

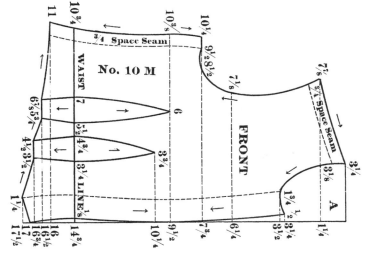

## LADIES' COSTUME.

Use the scale corresponding with the bust measure to draft the entire polonaise, which consists of two fronts, yoke, girdle and shirring, back, side back and sleeve.

Lay the pleats in the back according to the notches; take up the dart in the side back.

Turn down the front on the inside line and sew to the full front on the right side. Close the front on the left side with hooks and eyes; gather the sleeve between the notches. The front drapery is given on page 91. Draft by the waist measure. Lay the pleats according to the notches; drape up until it is even at the bottom of the skirt.

Use any plain skirt pattern for the foundation skirt. Trim to suit.

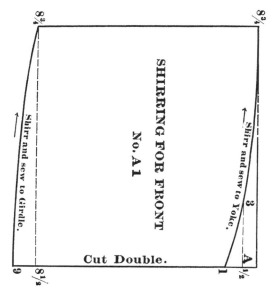

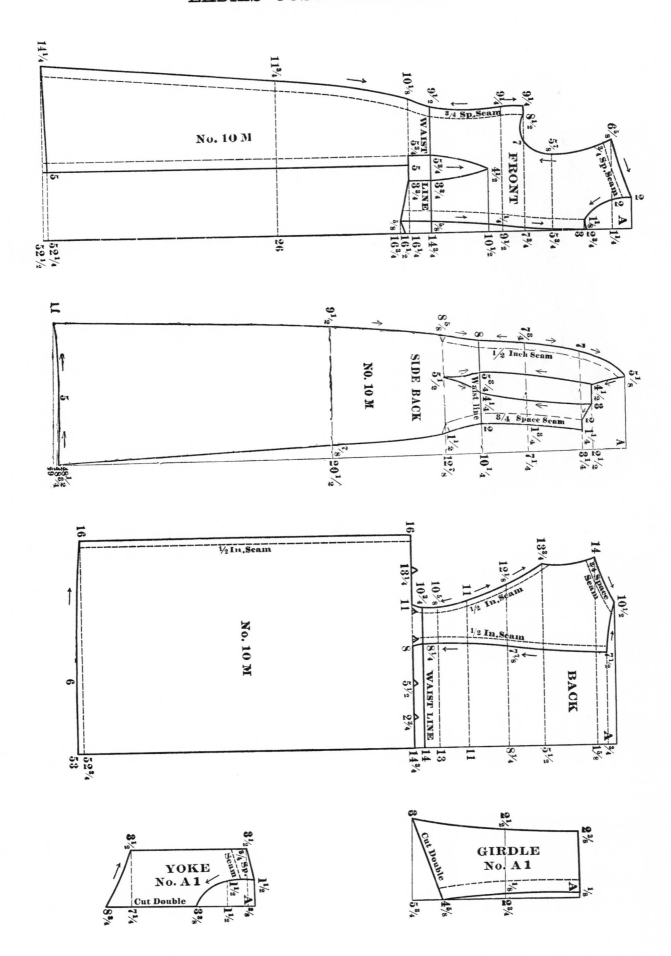

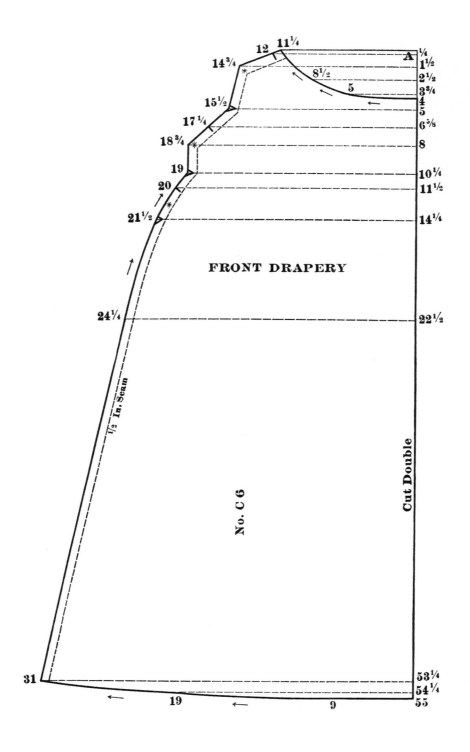

FRONT DRAPERY

No. C 6

Cut Double

1/2 In. Seam

# LADIES' EMPIRE GOWN.
## Spring 1893

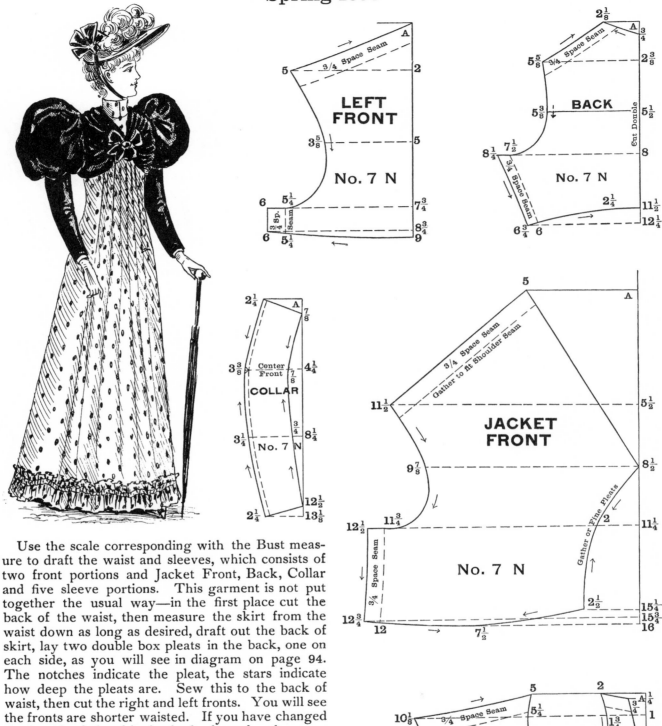

Use the scale corresponding with the Bust measure to draft the waist and sleeves, which consists of two front portions and Jacket Front, Back, Collar and five sleeve portions. This garment is not put together the usual way—in the first place cut the back of the waist, then measure the skirt from the waist down as long as desired, draft out the back of skirt, lay two double box pleats in the back, one on each side, as you will see in diagram on page 94. The notches indicate the pleat, the stars indicate how deep the pleats are. Sew this to the back of waist, then cut the right and left fronts. You will see the fronts are shorter waisted. If you have changed the length of the skirt in the back, make the same changes in front. Gather the front of the skirt and sew to the waist, then cut the jacket front, gather it on the shoulders between 5 on top base line and 11½ on first cross line, draw up to fit the shoulder, then join with under fronts and back in one seam, also join in the under arm seam; finish the front with a rosette of velvet or ornament.

The Sleeves are given on page 93. Cut the puffs and cuffs of velvet; cut the lining from the diagrams given. Draft the skirt from the waist measure.

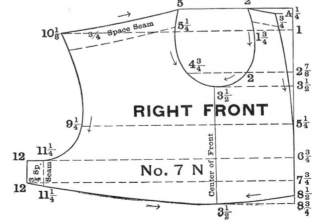

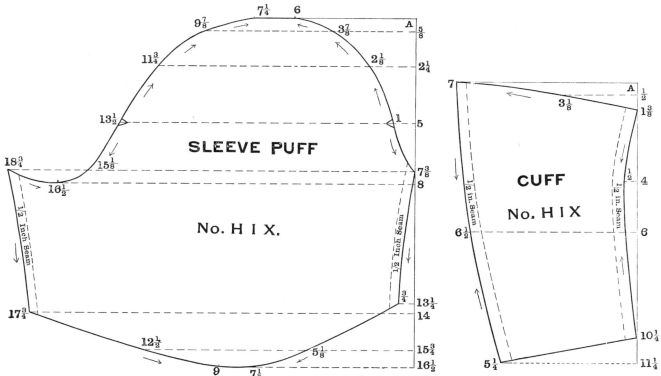

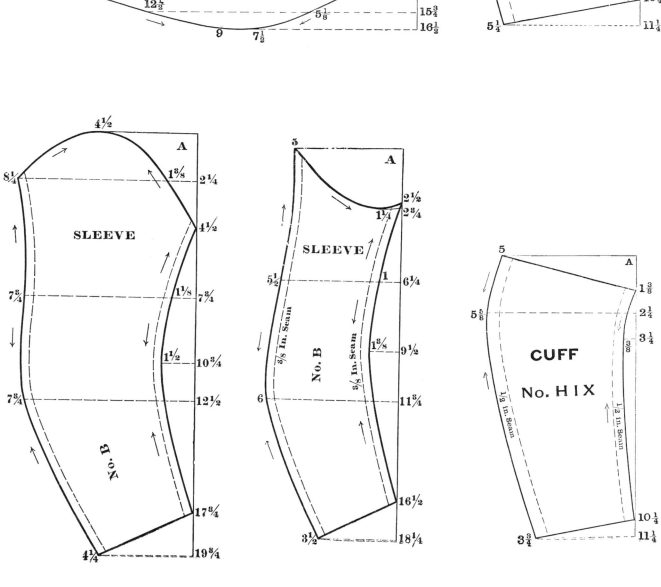

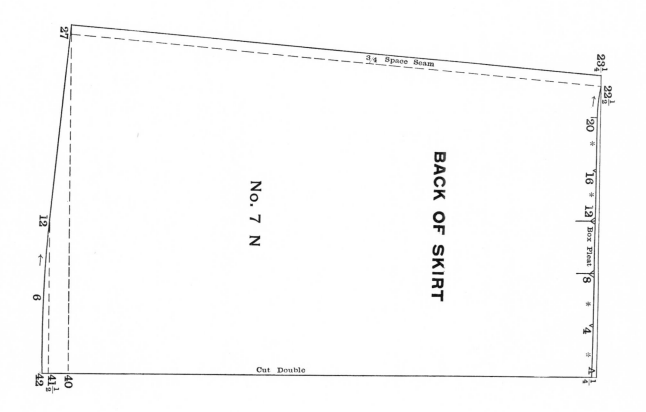

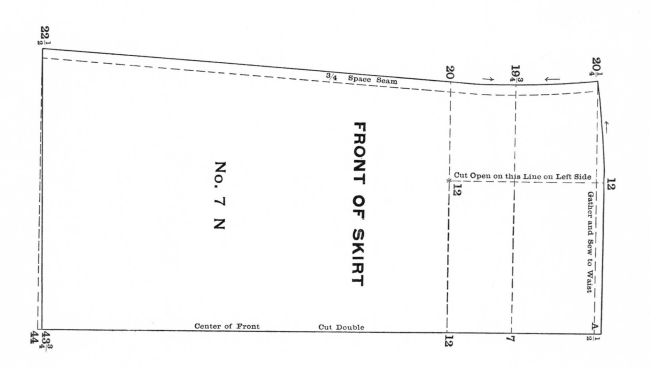

# LADIES' COSTUME.
## Summer 1893

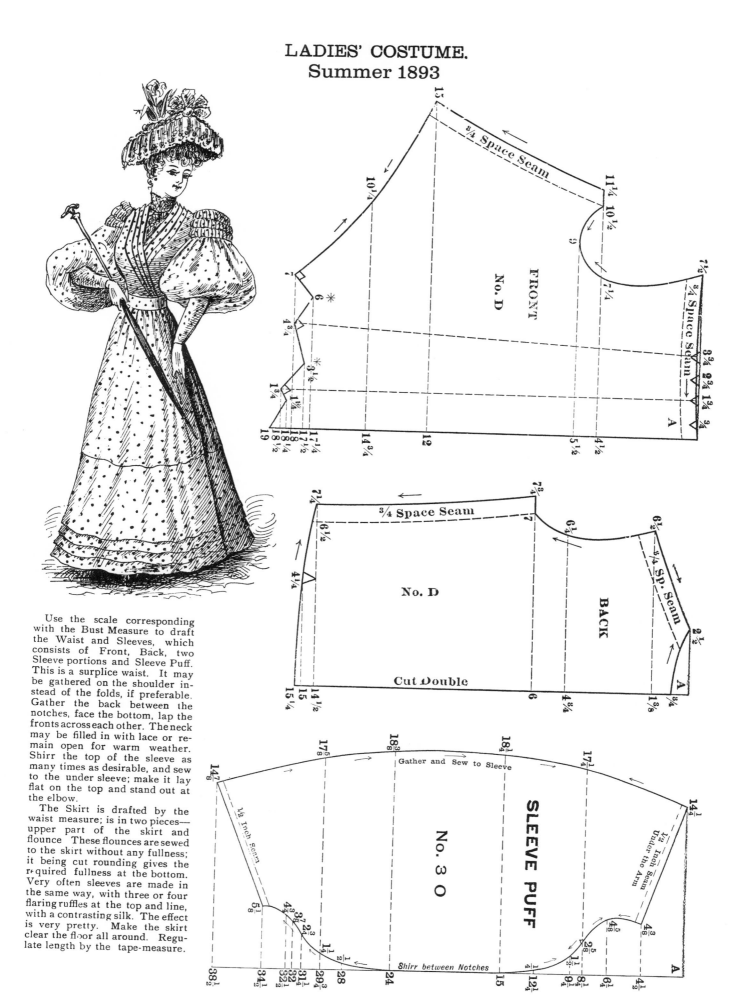

Use the scale corresponding with the Bust Measure to draft the Waist and Sleeves, which consists of Front, Back, two Sleeve portions and Sleeve Puff. This is a surplice waist. It may be gathered on the shoulder instead of the folds, if preferable. Gather the back between the notches, face the bottom, lap the fronts across each other. The neck may be filled in with lace or remain open for warm weather. Shirr the top of the sleeve as many times as desirable, and sew to the under sleeve; make it lay flat on the top and stand out at the elbow.

The Skirt is drafted by the waist measure; is in two pieces—upper part of the skirt and flounce These flounces are sewed to the skirt without any fullness; it being cut rounding gives the required fullness at the bottom. Very often sleeves are made in the same way, with three or four flaring ruffles at the top and line, with a contrasting silk. The effect is very pretty. Make the skirt clear the floor all around. Regulate length by the tape-measure.

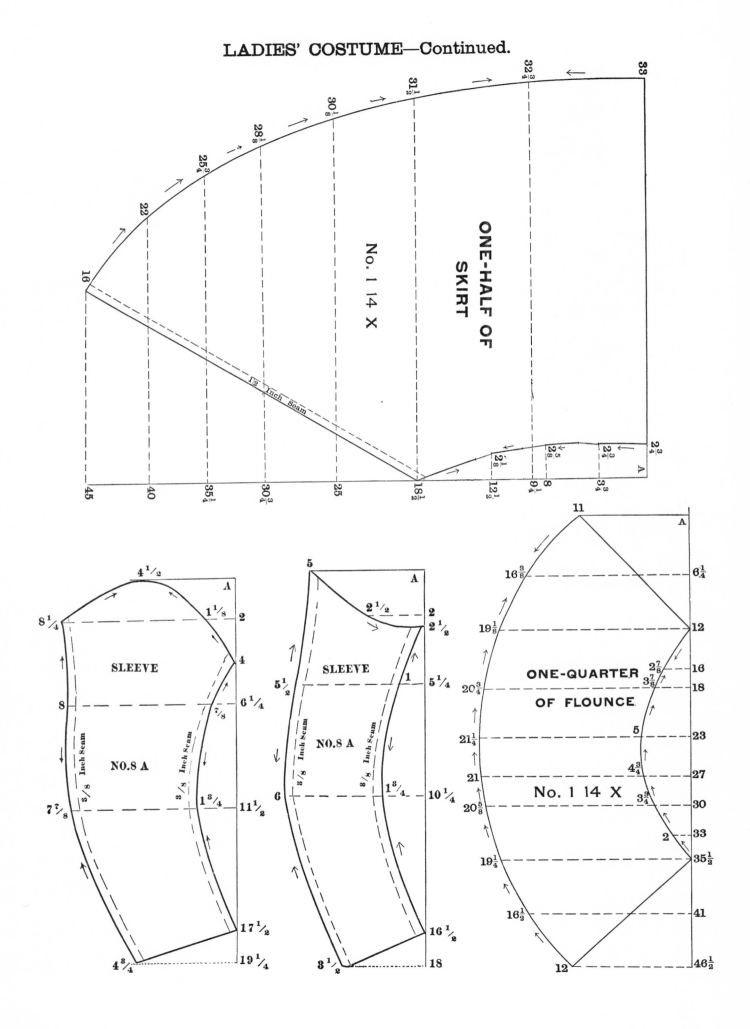

# LADIES' COSTUME.
## Summer 1893

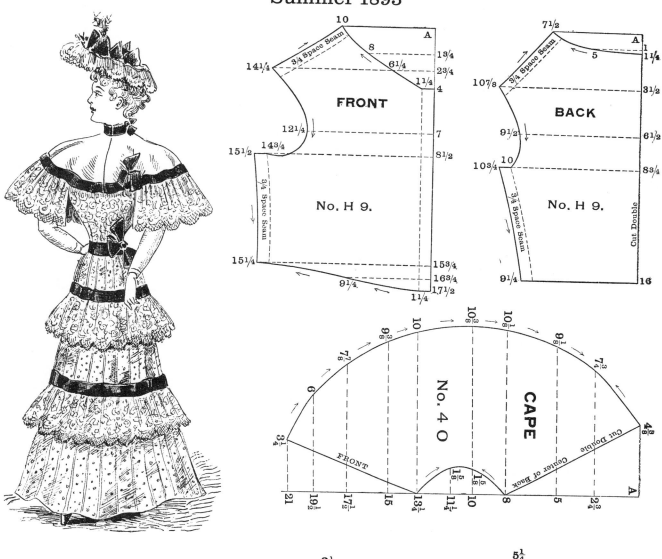

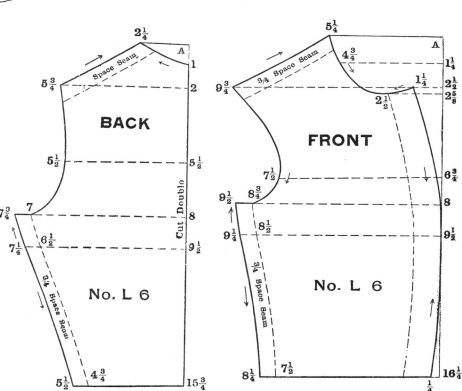

Use the scale corresponding with the Bust measure to draft the entire Waist and Cape, which consists of Front and Back for the Waist. Shirr as many times as desired at the neck, also gather at the Waist line. The Under Waist is in two pieces, Front and Back; the Cape is in one piece, cut double. Line with silk; trim the edge with lace. Use any Sleeve given in this issue. The Skirt is given on page 98. Draft by the Waist measure; is in two pieces, Front and Back; this gives the bell effect. Take up the darts, cut open and press; this may be gathered at the Waist, instead of the darts. Trim the Skirt to suit. Regulate the length by the tape measure.

# LADIES' COSTUME—Continued.

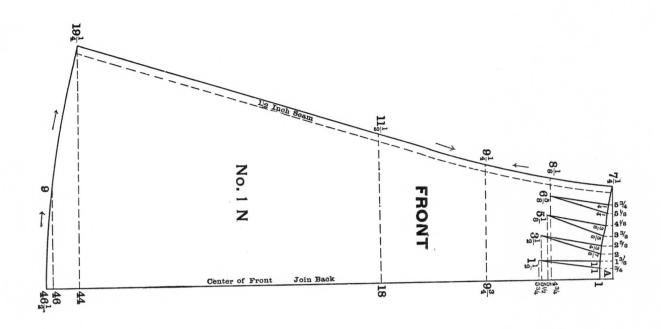

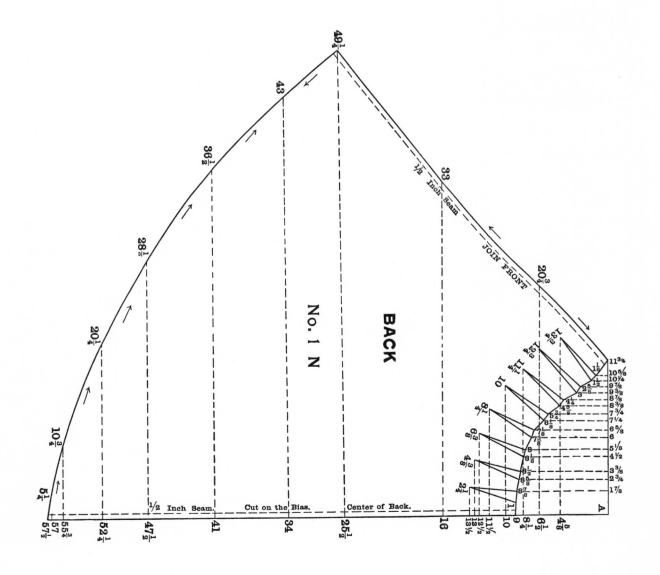

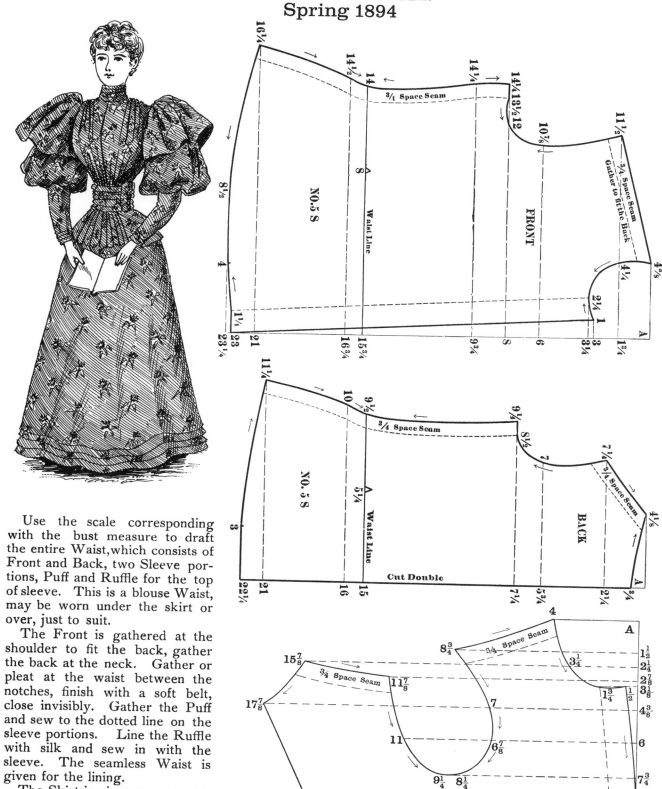

Use the scale corresponding with the bust measure to draft the entire Waist, which consists of Front and Back, two Sleeve portions, Puff and Ruffle for the top of sleeve. This is a blouse Waist, may be worn under the skirt or over, just to suit.

The Front is gathered at the shoulder to fit the back, gather the back at the neck. Gather or pleat at the waist between the notches, finish with a soft belt, close invisibly. Gather the Puff and sew to the dotted line on the sleeve portions. Line the Ruffle with silk and sew in with the sleeve. The seamless Waist is given for the lining.

The Skirt is given on page 101. Draft by the Waist measure. Is in three pieces, Front, Back and Side-gore. Gather the Back at the top. Trim the bottom with folds or any trimming desirable.

Regulate the length by the tape measure.

## ONE-HALF OF SEAMLESS WAIST

### No. 8 O

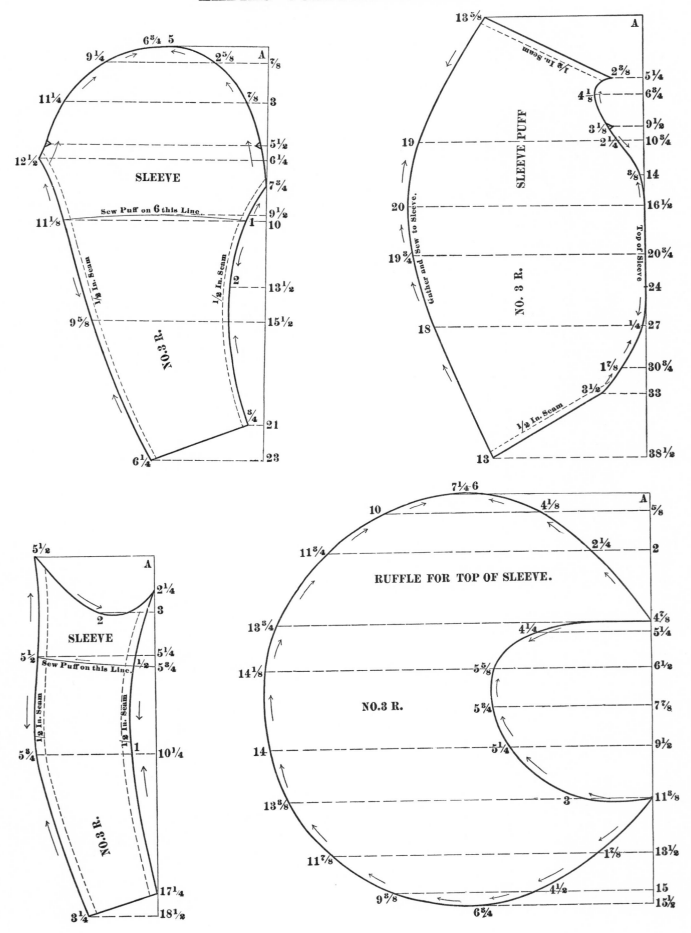

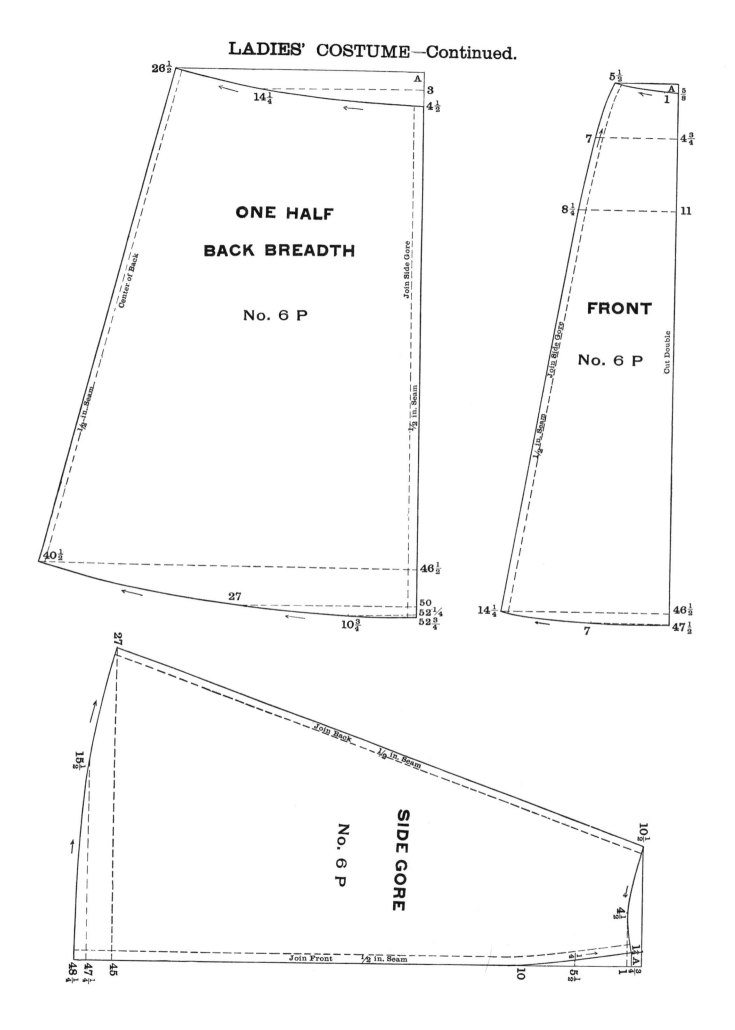

# LADIES' COSTUME
## Spring 1895

Use the scale corresponding with the bust measure to draft the entire waist, which consists of one-half of waist, rolling collar, vest, and standing collar, sleeve and skirt trimming.

This waist has no seams under the arm nor down the back. Take up the darts in front, close on the side with buttons and button holes, take up the shoulder seams, cut the rolling collar double, interline with canvas, and face with silk; sew to waist, trim with velvet.

Get the diagrams for the sleeves on page 104. Draft by the bust measure, lay the pleats to form a triple box pleat, finish the sleeve trimming all around and place upon this box pleat, tack it in place. Use the diagrams for the skirt, on pages 62 and 63. Draft by the waist measure, interline throughout with grasscloth, face up the bottom with velvet, place the skirt trimming on each side as represented.

The vest is made of linen. Use this diagram for the lining, lay a side pleat down the center of the outside.

Finish with a standing collar.

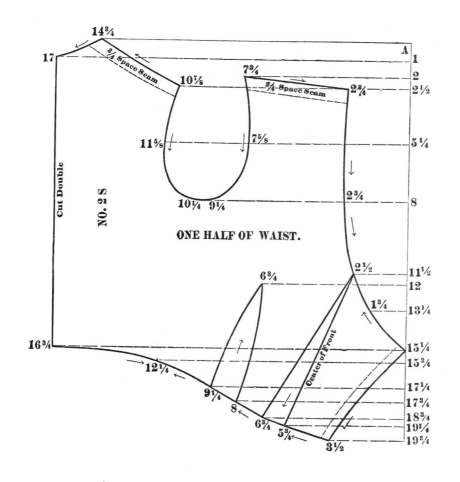

ONE HALF OF WAIST.

NO. 2 S

Cut Double

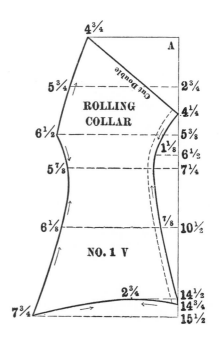

ROLLING COLLAR

Cut Double

NO. 1 V

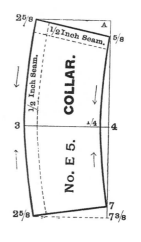

COLLAR.

No. E 5.

1/2 Inch Seam.

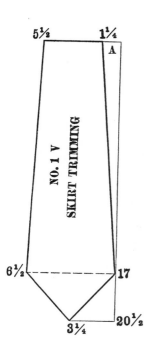

NO. 1 V
SKIRT TRIMMING

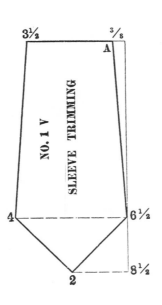

NO. 1 V
SLEEVE TRIMMING

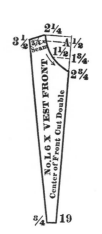

No. L 6 X VEST FRONT
Center of Front Cut Double

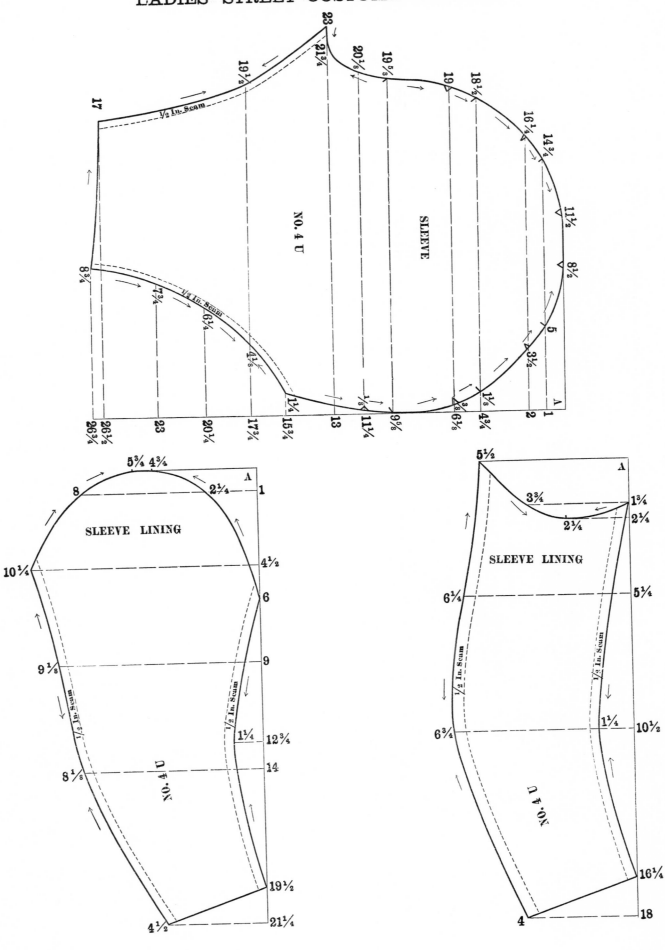

# LADIES' HOUSE DRESS.
## Spring 1895

Use the scale corresponding with the bust measure to draft the entire waist. This is a seamless waist, and surely is a novelty. There are no visible seams whatever. The back extends over to the front, and forms a yoke. Tack the front shoulder on the dotted line on shoulder (see diagram). Connect the stars and rings. Take up the dart over the bust; cut open and press carefully; the yoke will cover it. Close down the front invisibly with hooks and eyes. When the pattern is drafted out, if too small, change in front at 2¼, one-half the desired amount. Do not attempt to use this for a stout form. The bottom may be finished with a soft fold of velvet, the same to be used to finish bottom of yoke, and crush collar. Bone the lining same as any other waist.

The Umbrella skirt is drafted by the waist measure, is in one piece. Take all the extra fullness to the back. Interline with grass cloth, and face the bottom with velvet.

Regulate the length by the tape measure.

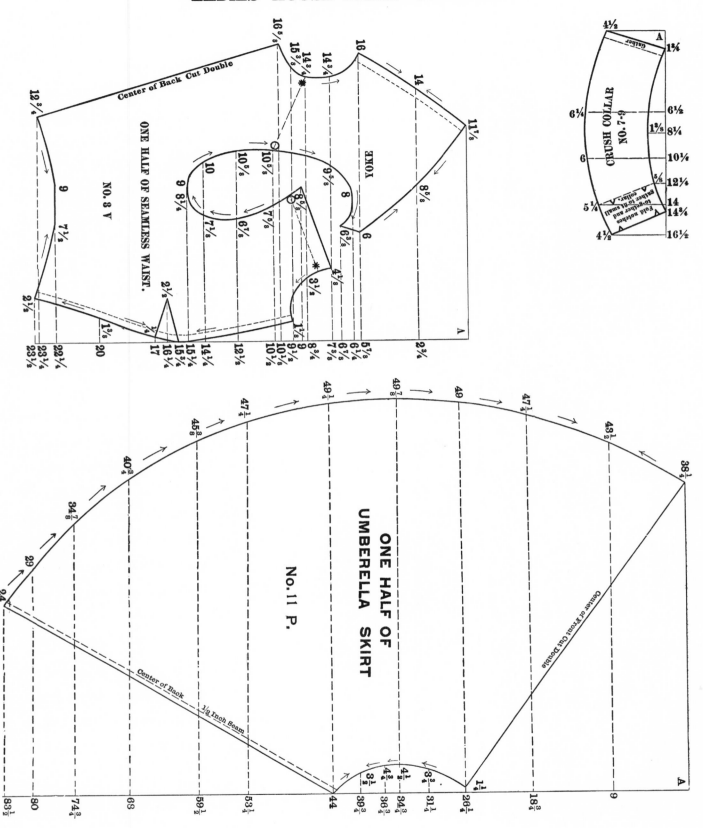

ONE HALF OF SEAMLESS WAIST.

NO. 3 V

YOKE

Center of Back Cut Double

CRUSH COLLAR
NO. 7-9

ONE HALF OF
UMBERELLA SKIRT

No. 11 P.

Center of Back

½ Inch Seam

Center of Front Cut Double

# YOUNG LADIES' HOUSE DRESS.
## Spring 1895

Use the scale corresponding with the bust measure to draft the entire waist, which consists of two front yokes and two back yokes, and shirring for front and back. The full portions may be made of velvet or silk. Sew to the plain yoke, gather the bottom and sew to a belt.

The pointed yoke is embroidered, or may be made of velvet, edged with jet, and the full portions made of same material as the dress. Finish the neck with a stock collar; also finish the waist with a soft twist of velvet, and bow at the side.

Use the sleeves on pages 65 and 66, or any other more desirable pattern.

Use the skirt given on page 106. Draft by the waist measure. Bring all the fullness in the back. Trim with velvet bands, or any other style.

Regulate the length by the tape measure.

# LADIES' HOUSE DRESS—Continued.

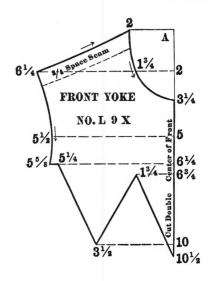

FRONT YOKE NO. L 9 X

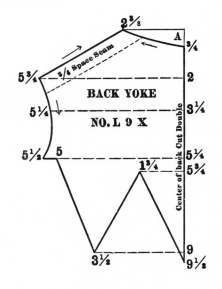

BACK YOKE NO. L 9 X

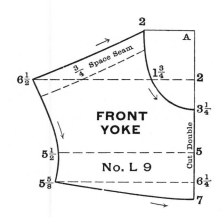

FRONT YOKE No. L 9

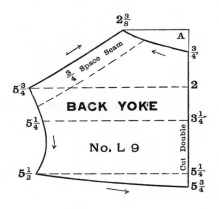

BACK YOKE No. L 9

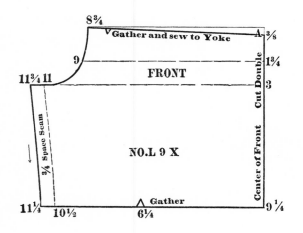

FRONT NO. L 9 X

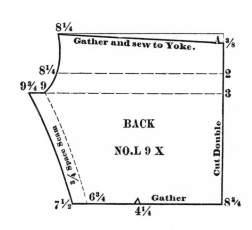

BACK NO. L 9 X

# LADIES' COSTUME.
## Spring 1895

Use the scale corresponding with the bust measure to draft the entire waist, jacket and sleeves. The waist consists of two fronts, two backs and three sleeve portions. Gather the upper portion at neck and waist line. This gives the blouse effect in front, and may be made of silk or any thin material. The jacket is seamless, except the shoulder seams. Draft same as any other garment. Line throughout with silk. The rolling collar is given on page 110. It gives the sailor back and straight front. Keep in place with a twist of velvet and rosettes at each side. Use the crush collar on page 106. Interline the puff for the sleeve with tarletan or cross-bar canvas and gather or pleat, and sew to the tight sleeve on dotted line.

The bell skirt is drafted by the waist measure, is in one piece. Interline with grass cloth, and face with velvet.

Trim with graduated lengths of velvet and bows.

Regulate the length by the tape measure.

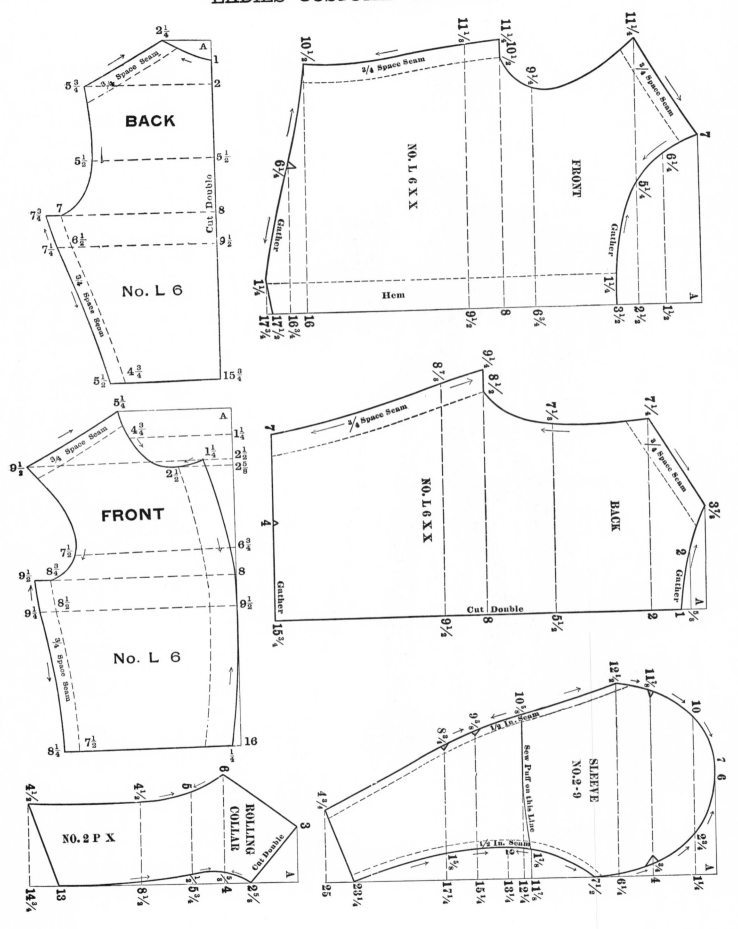

## LADIES' COSTUME.

Use the scale corresponding with the bust measure to draft the entire waist and sleeves, which consists of two Fronts, Back, Vest Front, Rolling Sailor Collar, Neck Band, and small Rolling Collar, Cuff and three Sleeve portions.

The Back may be made with or without a seam down the center. Cut the lining from the Front having two Darts. Close with hooks and eyes. Cut the Vest, or center Front, double, sew to the lining on the right Side, and fasten on the left Side with hooks and eyes. Sew the large Rolling Collar to the upper Front and tack to the lining on the right Side and close invisibly with hooks and eyes. Interline the Rolling Collar with Tailors' Canvas. The French Sleeve may be made, as it now shows, with pleats coming just below the elbow, finished with a fancy cuff, or the figures 18¾ and 19½ may be lowered nearly to the bottom, which would give the Bishop Sleeve effect. In either case, the top of the Sleeve should be lined with fibre chamois or light weight canvas, or sea grass, the latter being the favorite.

The Skirt is given on page 114. Draft by the waist measure. Line it with cotton taffeta or the old fashioned paper cambric, trim the entire garment with velvet and braid or jet.

Regulate the length by the tape measure.

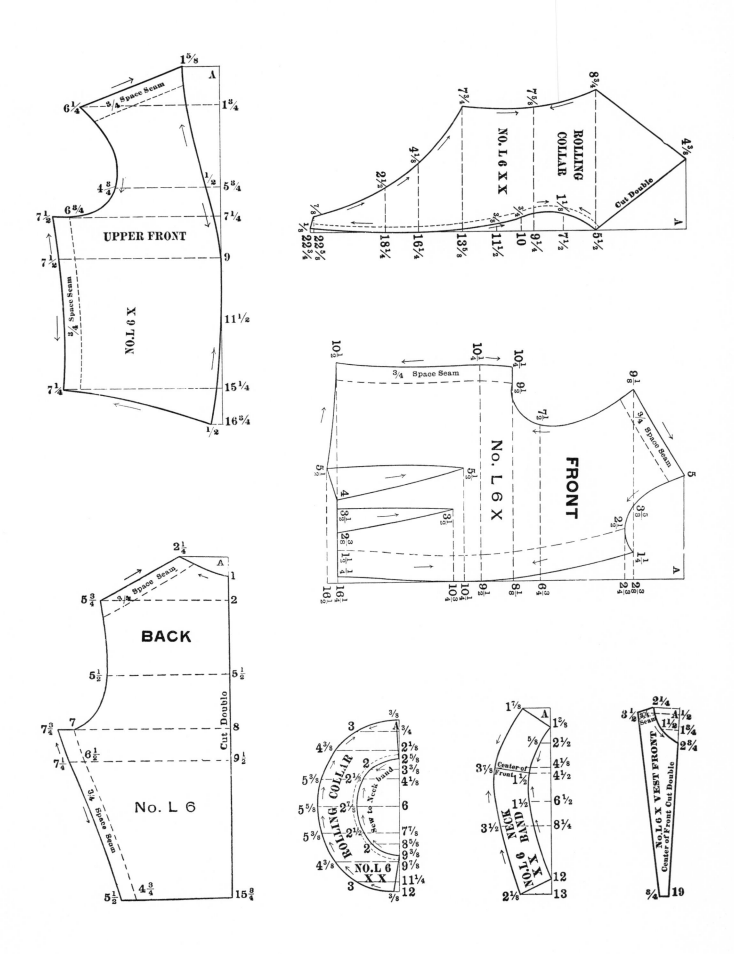

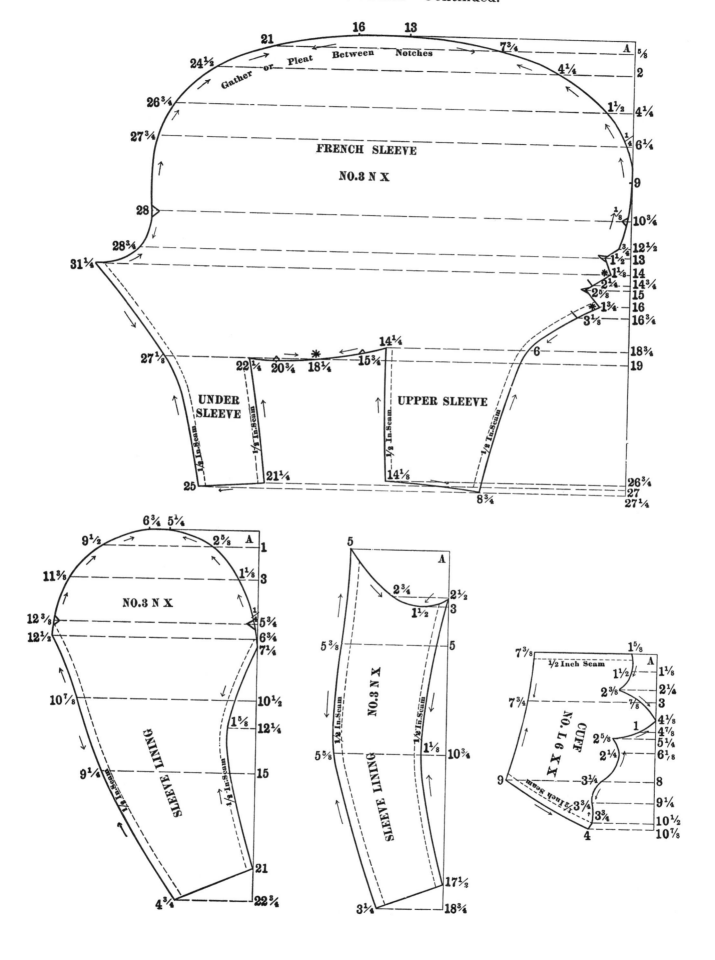

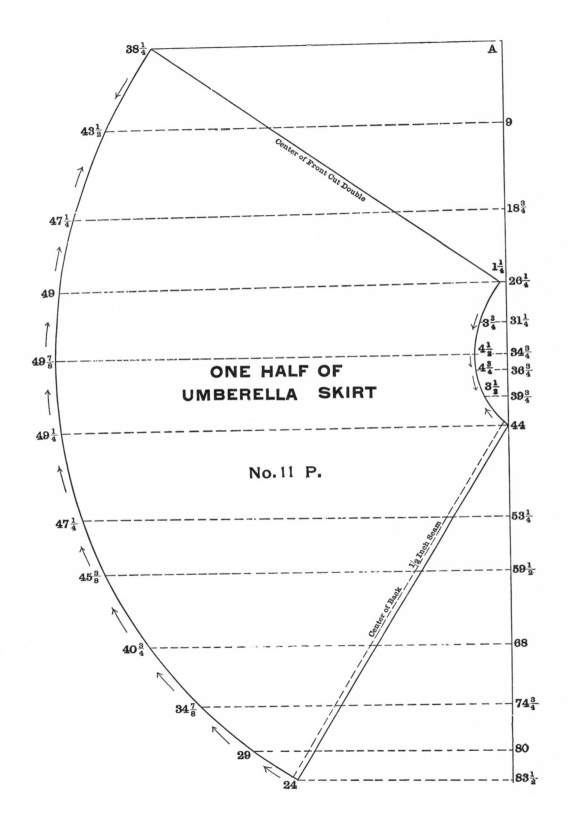

**ONE HALF OF
UMBERELLA SKIRT**

No. 11 P.

### LADIES' COSTUME.

Use the scale corresponding with the Bust measure. It consists of two Fronts, two Backs, two Yoke pieces and three Sleeve portions. Cut the lining only from the smallest Front and Back, gather the upper portions at the Neck and Waist and sew to the lining; close down the center invisibly. Make the Yoke of same material as the Sleeves; trim with passementerie or braid; close on the left shoulder with hooks and loops; gather the Sleeve Puff and sew to the Sleeve; interline as we have already explained. Use the Skirt on Page 114.

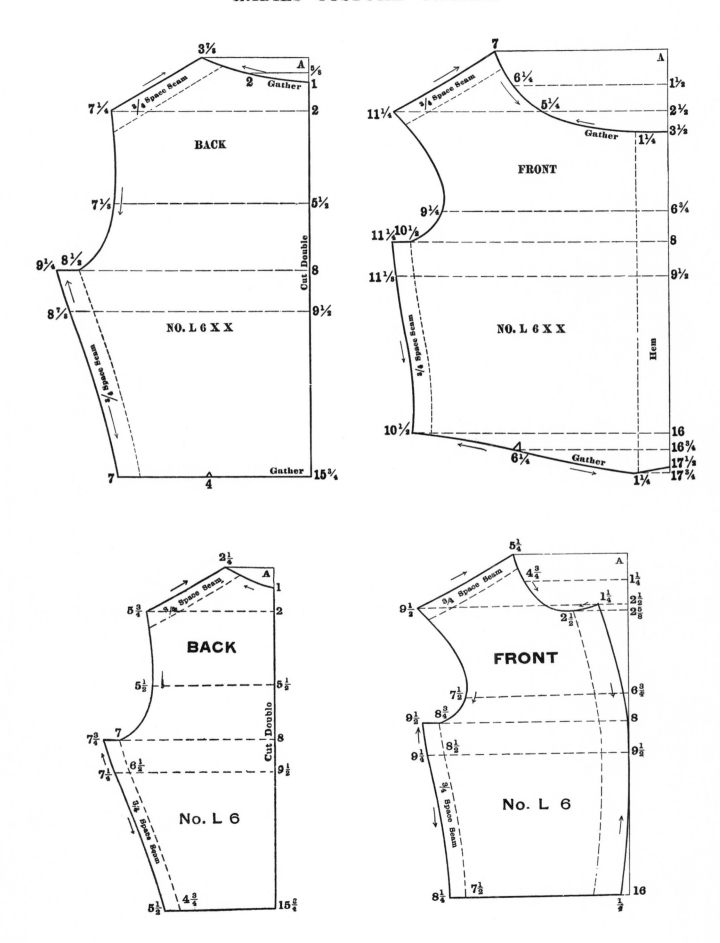

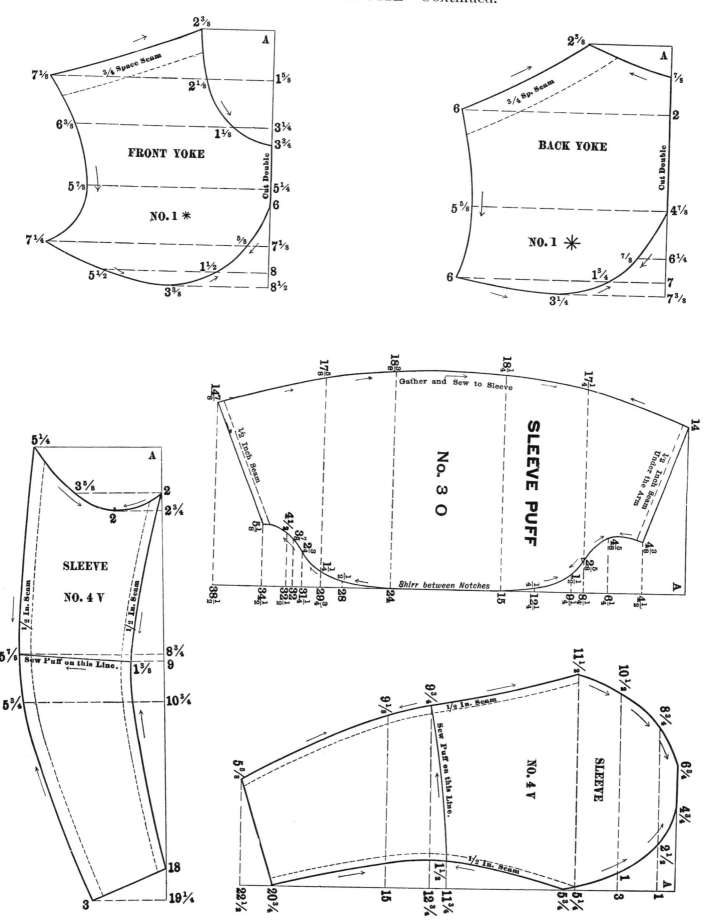

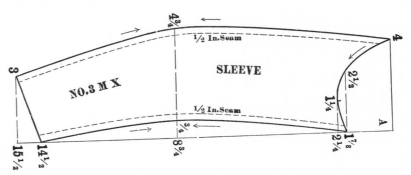

## STOUT LADIES' PRINCESS.

(This has been inserted by special request.)

Use the scale corresponding with the bust measure to draft the entire garment, which consists of Front, Back, Side-back, two Under-arm gores, Collar and two Sleeve portions.

Draft same as all other garments; lay pleats in the back; join the under-arm gores according to the stars.

The ruffle over the shoulder may be carried to a sharp point in the back, same as the front, or it may be omitted just to suit. Close in front with hooks and eyes. Any style of trimming may be used.

Regulate the length by the tape measure.

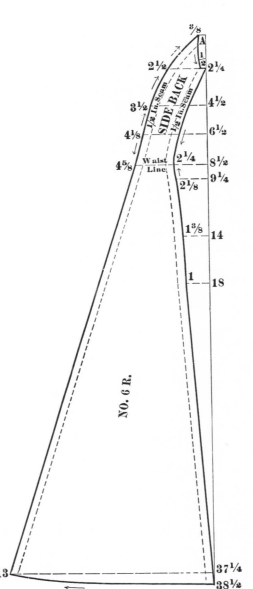

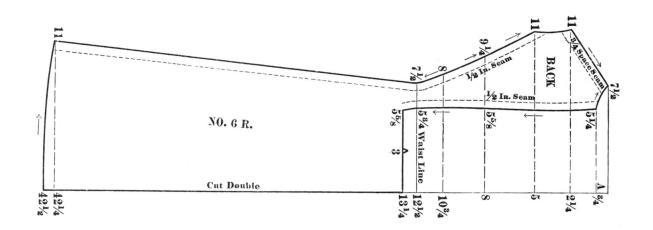

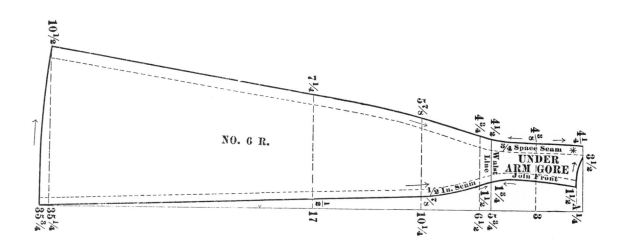

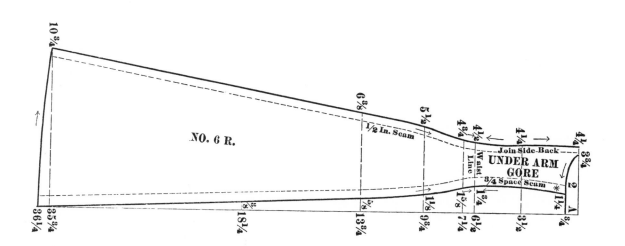

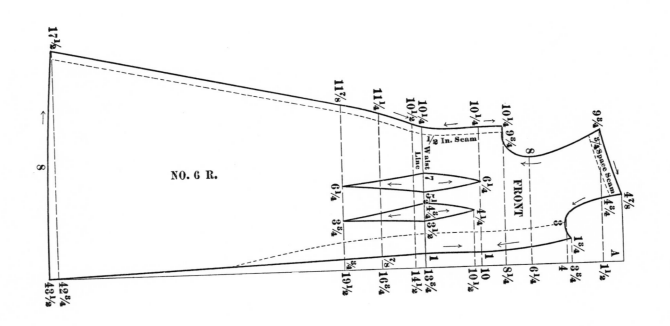

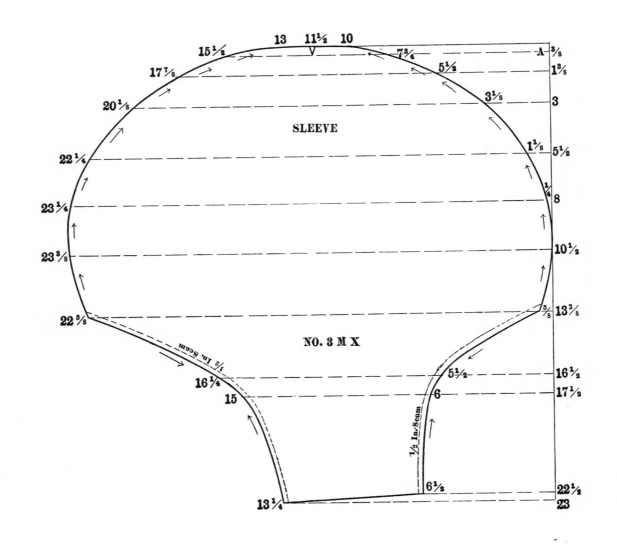

# LADIES' TIGHT-FITTING JACKET.
## Winter 1890-91

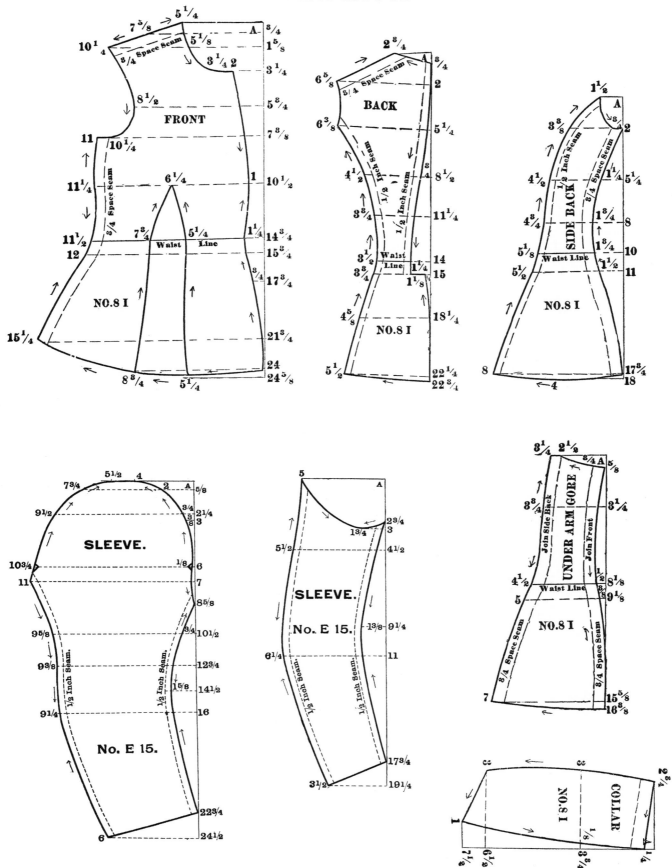

# LADIES' HUNTER'S JACKET.
## Spring 1895

Use the scale corresponding with the bust measure to draft the entire waist, which consists of front, back, and collar.

Lay the pleats according to the notches, two box pleats in front and two in the back. It may be made of silk or cloth. Hem the bottom.

The sleeves are given on pages 65 and 66. Draft by the bust measure. Be sure and interline the puff with Tarletan or cross-barred canvas. Lay the pleats according to the notches, forming three double-box pleats. Sew up the seam and gather the bottom, and sew to the lining. Finish with a soft roll of velvet and bows.

Draft the skirt from the diagram given on page 67. Use the scale corresponding with the waist measure. Face the bottom with heavy canvas, and bind it with velvet. We have omitted some of the skirts and sleeves for want of room.

Regulate the length by the tape measure.

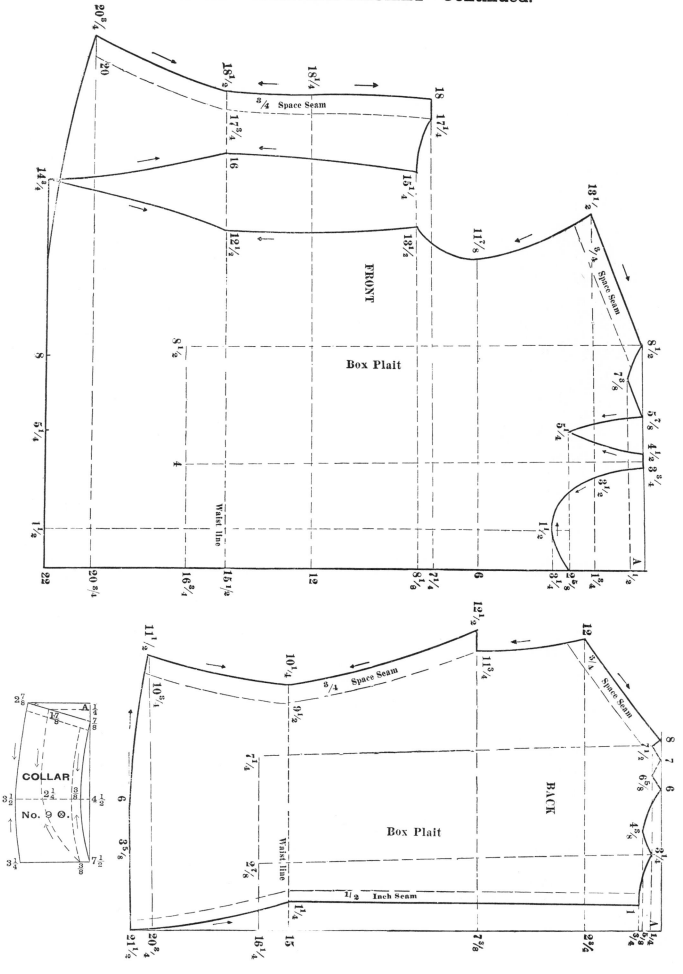

# TENNIS COSTUME.
## Fall 1890

*TENNIS COSTUME.*

Use the scale corresponding with the bust measure to draft the jacket and waist. The jacket consists of Back, Side Back, Under Arm-gore, and two Sleeve portions.

Face the front back as far as the diagonal line; turn this back to form a rolling collar. Finish the edge with a gold or silver cord. The blouse or shirt waist consists of front, back, collar, cuff, sleeve facing and sleeve. Tuck the front as represented, close with buttons. Face the bottom and insert a cord. The under waist is given on page 126; Is in three pieces: Front, Back and Side Back.

Draft the skirt by the waist measure; lay the pleats according to the notches. Press carefully and sew to the under waist. Regulate the length by the tape measure.

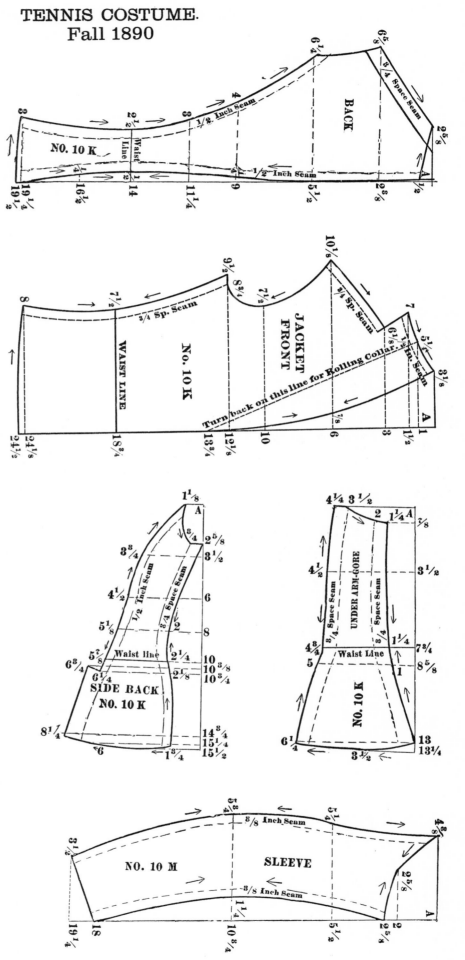

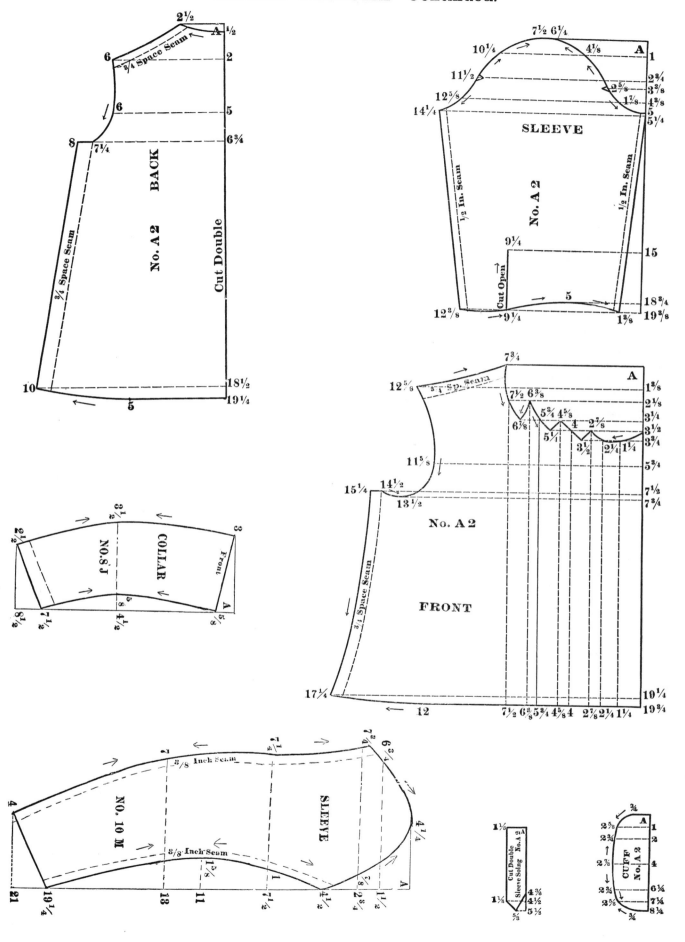

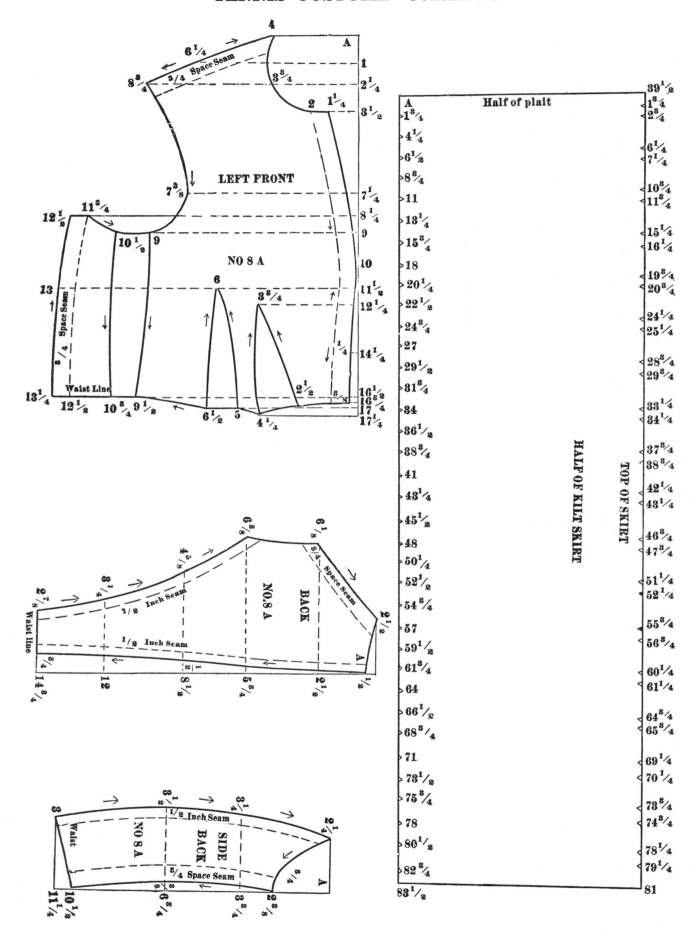

# RIDING HABIT.
## Spring 1891

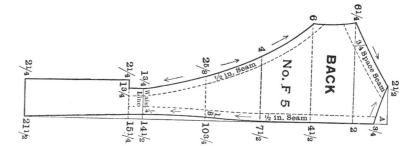

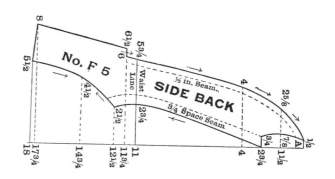

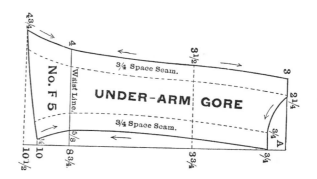

Use the scale corresponding with the Bust measure to draft the entire Basque, which consists of Front, Back, Side-back, Under-arm Gore, Collar and two Sleeve portions. Draft and make up the same as all other Basques.

The Skirt is given on pages 128 and 129. Draft by the scale corresponding with the Waist measure. Take up the darts as represented. Put the parts together according to the stars and notches. Finish the bottom with a wide hem. When off the horse, loop up the skirt to walking length with a cord attached to the waist-band.

Regulate the length by the tape measure.

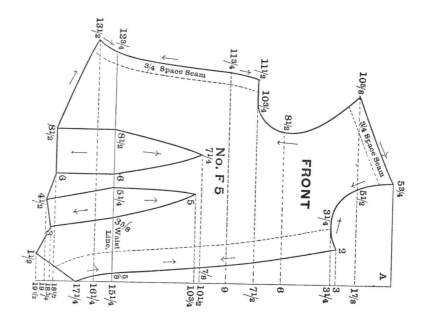

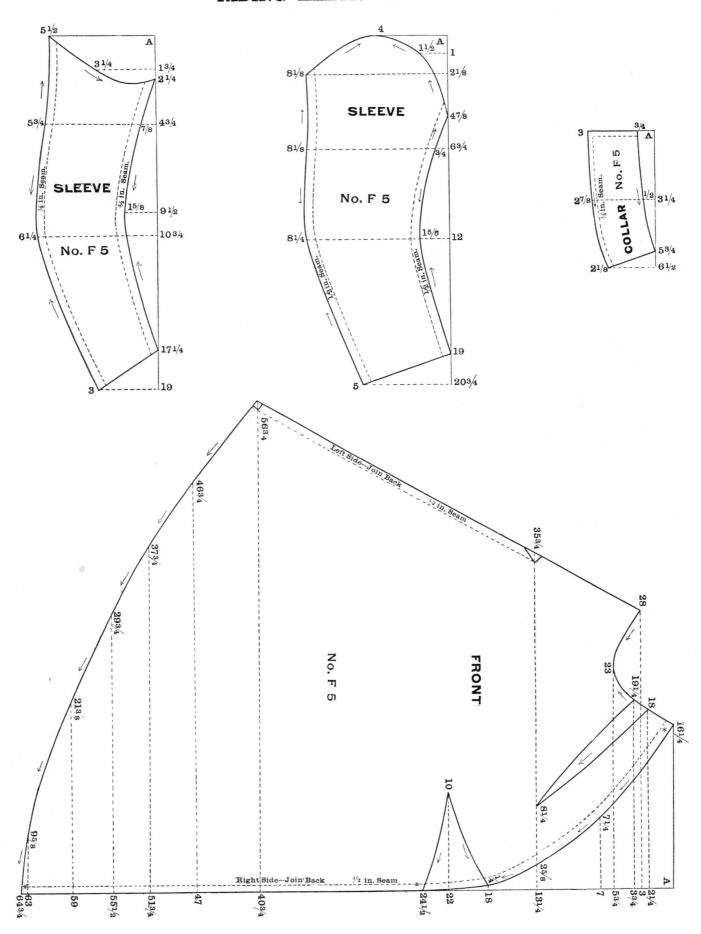

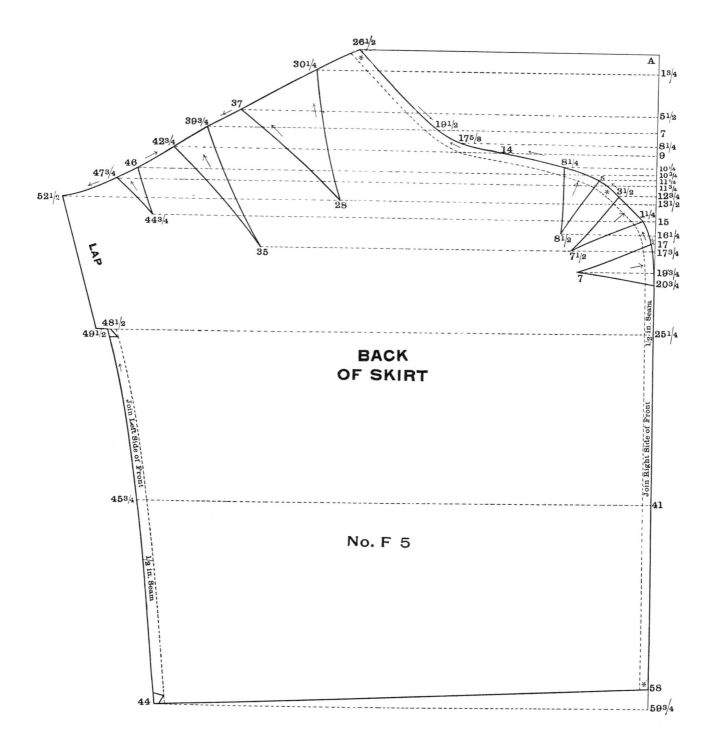

**BACK
OF SKIRT**

No. F 5

LAP

# YOUNG LADIES' EVENING COSTUME.
## Spring 1891

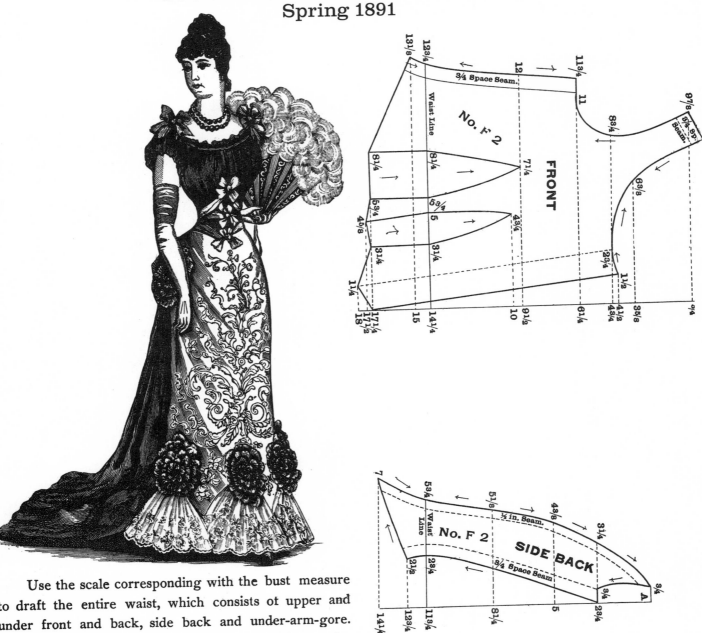

Use the scale corresponding with the bust measure to draft the entire waist, which consists ot upper and under front and back, side back and under-arm-gore. Turn down the upper front and back and shirr on the second dotted line. Lay the pleats at the bottom according to the notches. Sew the under back and side back together before basting the upper back on.

The sleeves are simply a piece of lace or same material as the waist gathered very full on the top, caught up with a bow of ribbons or rozette to correspond with the skirt. The diagram for the skirt is shown on page 132. Use the scale corresponding with the waist measure. It consists of back and front. Lay the pleats according to the notches, making the skirt the desired length in front. The back is simply side pleats turning towards the center of the back. This may be made entirely separate from the skirt proper if preferred. Regulate the length by the tape measure.

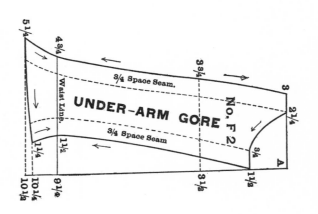

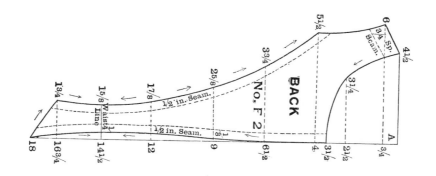

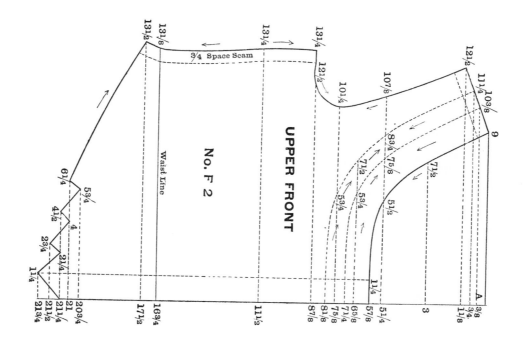

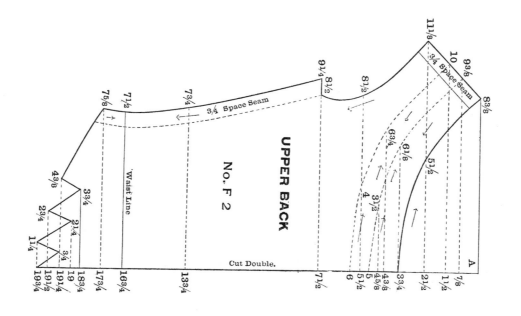

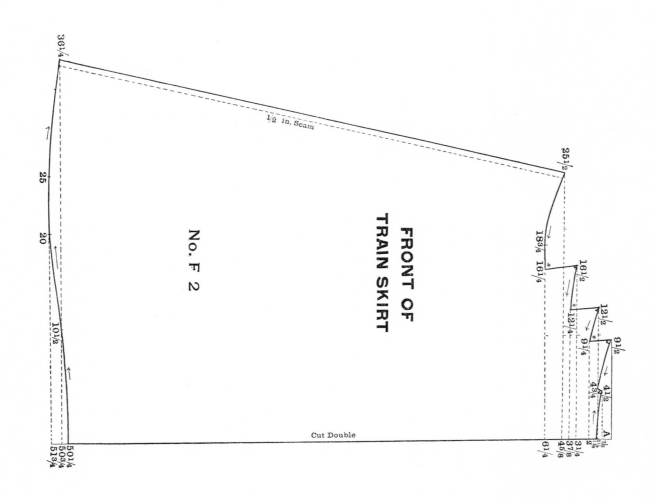

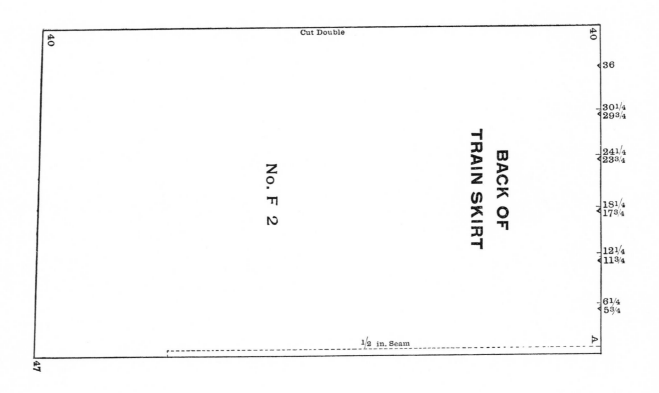

# LADIES' EVENING GOWN.
## Spring 1894

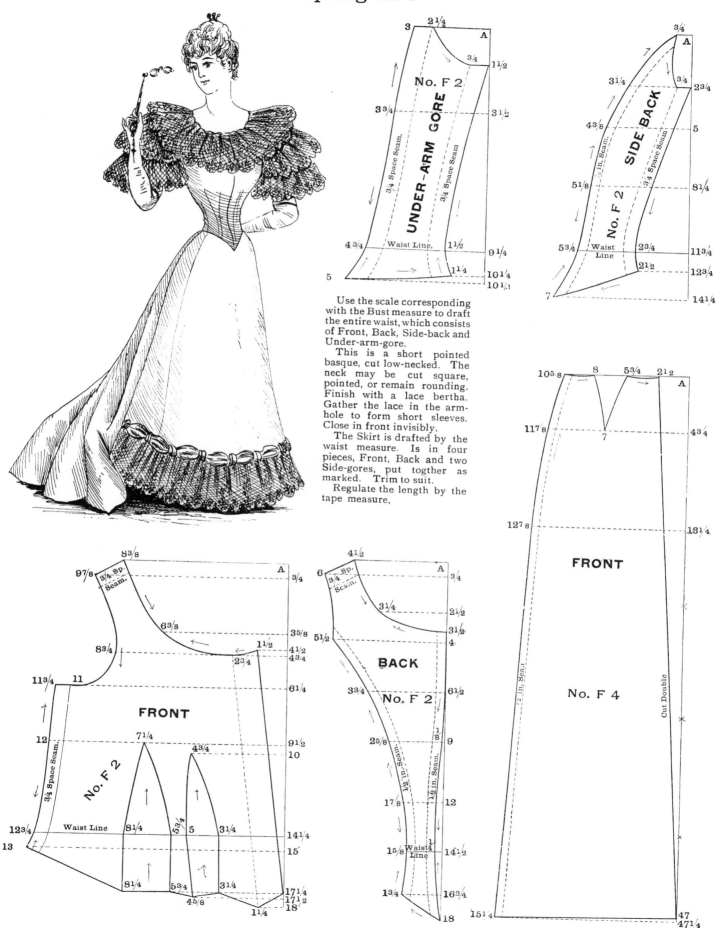

Use the scale corresponding with the Bust measure to draft the entire waist, which consists of Front, Back, Side-back and Under-arm-gore.

This is a short pointed basque, cut low-necked. The neck may be cut square, pointed, or remain rounding. Finish with a lace bertha. Gather the lace in the armhole to form short sleeves. Close in front invisibly.

The Skirt is drafted by the waist measure. Is in four pieces, Front, Back and two Side-gores, put togther as marked. Trim to suit.

Regulate the length by the tape measure,

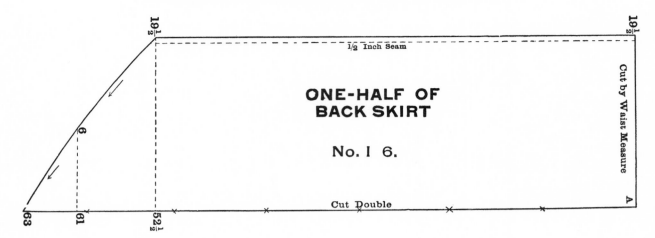

**ONE-HALF OF BACK SKIRT**

No. I 6.

1/2 Inch Seam

Cut by Waist Measure

Cut Double

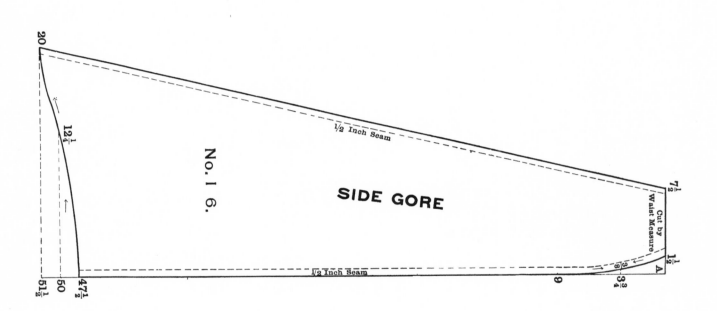

No. I 6.

**SIDE GORE**

1/2 Inch Seam

1/2 Inch Seam

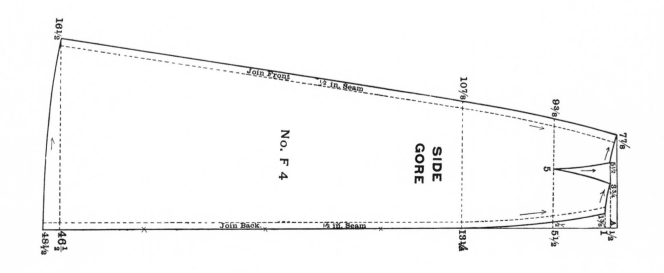

Join Front 1/2 in. Seam

No. F 4

**SIDE GORE**

Join Back. 1/2 in. Seam

# LADIES' SACK NIGHTDRESS.
## Winter 1890-91

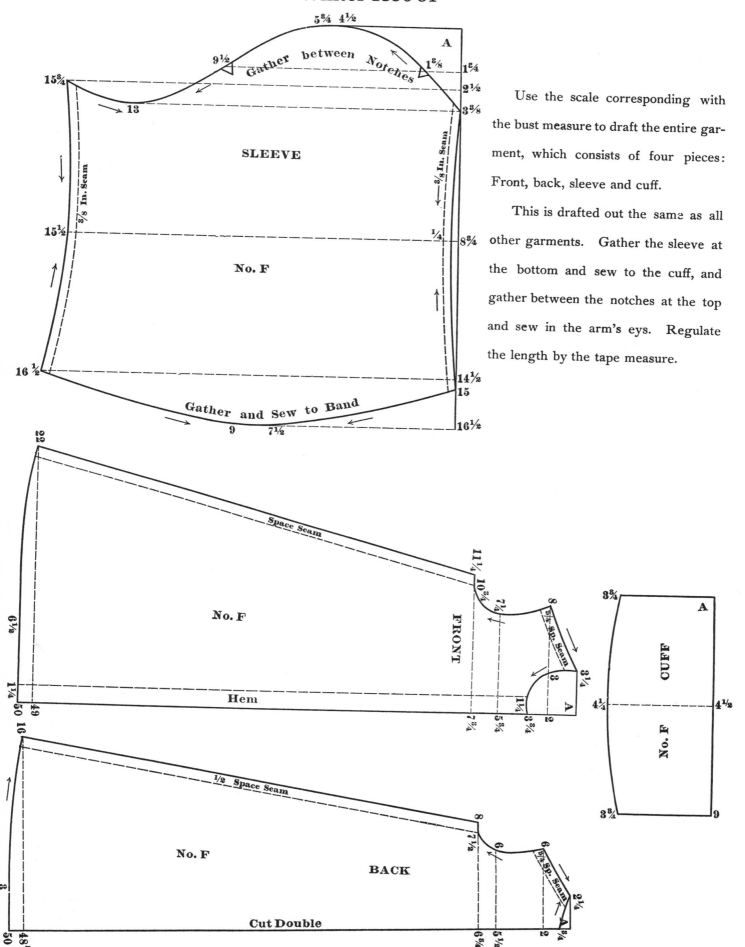

Use the scale corresponding with the bust measure to draft the entire garment, which consists of four pieces: Front, back, sleeve and cuff.

This is drafted out the same as all other garments. Gather the sleeve at the bottom and sew to the cuff, and gather between the notches at the top and sew in the arm's eys. Regulate the length by the tape measure.

# LADIES' NIGHT GOWN.
## Spring 1893

**Ladies' Half Fitting Night Gown.**

Use the scale corresponding with the Bust measure to draft the entire garment which consists of Front, Back, two Yoke portions, Collar, Sleeve and Cuff.

Trim the lower part of the Yoke with embroidery, also bring it over the shoulder, sew it in with the sleeve. The effect is very pretty. The Yoke may be made of tucks and insertion. Trim the Collar with embroidery also.

Regulate the length by the tape-measure.

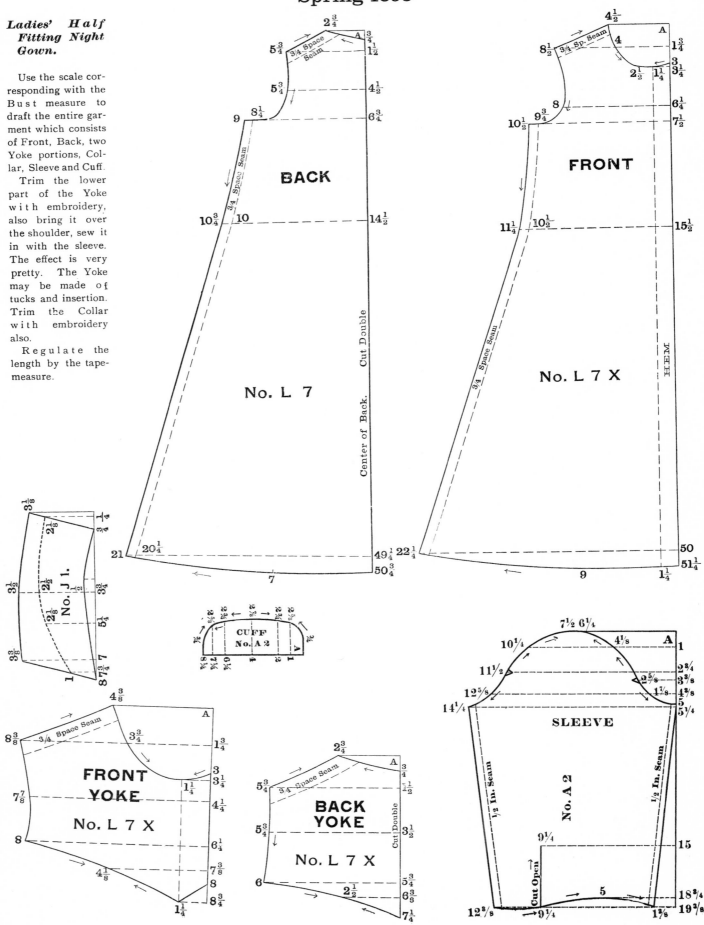

BACK

No. L 7

FRONT

No. L 7 X

No. J 1.

CUFF No. A 2

FRONT YOKE
No. L 7 X

BACK YOKE
No. L 7 X

SLEEVE
No. A 2